PHOTOSHOP ELEMENTS
Express

ANDREW BECKLEY
MARILENE OLIVER

friendsof

DESIGNER TO DESIGNER™

PHOTOSHOP ELEMENTS
Express

© 2002 friends of ED

First published March 2002

Trademark Acknowledgments

friends of ED has endeavored to provide trademark information about all the companies and products mentioned in this book by the appropriate use of capitals. However, friends of ED cannot guarantee the accuracy of this information.

Published by friends of ED
30-32 Lincoln Road, Olton, Birmingham. B27 6PA. UK.

Printed in USA

ISBN: 1-903450-54-3

PHOTOSHOP ELEMENTS *Express*

CREDITS

AUTHORS
CHAPTERS: MARILENE OLIVER
ANDREW BECKLEY

DESIGNERS: GAVIN CROMHOUT
JIM HANNAH

TECHNICAL REVIEWERS
ALEXANDRA BLACKBURN
DARYL CLEWLOW
DENIS E. GRAHAM
WILLIAM MCINTYRE
ERIC SMOLLIN
MICHAEL WALSTON

PROOF READERS
JON BOUNDS
JULIE CLOSS
ADAM DUTTON

INDEXER
FIONA MURRAY

COMMISSIONING EDITOR
ADAM JUNIPER

EDITORS
CAROLINE ROBESON

AUTHOR AGENT
MEL JEHS

PROJECT MANAGER
SIMON BRAND

GRAPHIC EDITORS
MATTHEW CLARK
WILLIAM FALLON

COVER DESIGN
KATY FREER

MANAGING EDITOR
CHRIS HINDLEY

Marilene Oliver MA RCA www.marilene.co.uk
Born in Essex, England in 1977. Studied Fine Art
Printmaking and Photomedia at Central Saint Martins
School of Art and Design, London before going on to do
an MA in Fine Art Printmaking at the Royal College of Art,
London.

She now works as a Fine Artist in London. Her work seeks
to address how new technologies such as medical
imaging and electronic communication systems are
affecting the intimate and sensual body. She has
exhibited extensively in London and is currently working
towards a solo show with Beaux Arts Gallery. She also
works as a digital/print assistant at the Royal College of
Art, London.

Andrew Beckley. www.shelfstacker.org

00:00. Registration and coffee. Told to outline ideas and put together geometry, images and sound to go into our environment. There was a virtual space which acted as a gateway for the spaces you built.

00:11. Short film shown. This will open your eyes.

00:11. Discussion about how far we got on and what additional support is needed. The real space is a large shared room, which is partitioned into individual or group spaces according to your needs. Initially the virtual space reflects the real space but you are free to change this once you go off on your own.

06:00. Not too much is decided about what happens now.

18:00. Shown to accommodation

23:59. You may continue to work on or leave at this point

I thought that we might go for a picnic at some point this evening if the weather is good.

TABLE OF CONTENTS

4. Text and Effects   91

5. Shapes   109

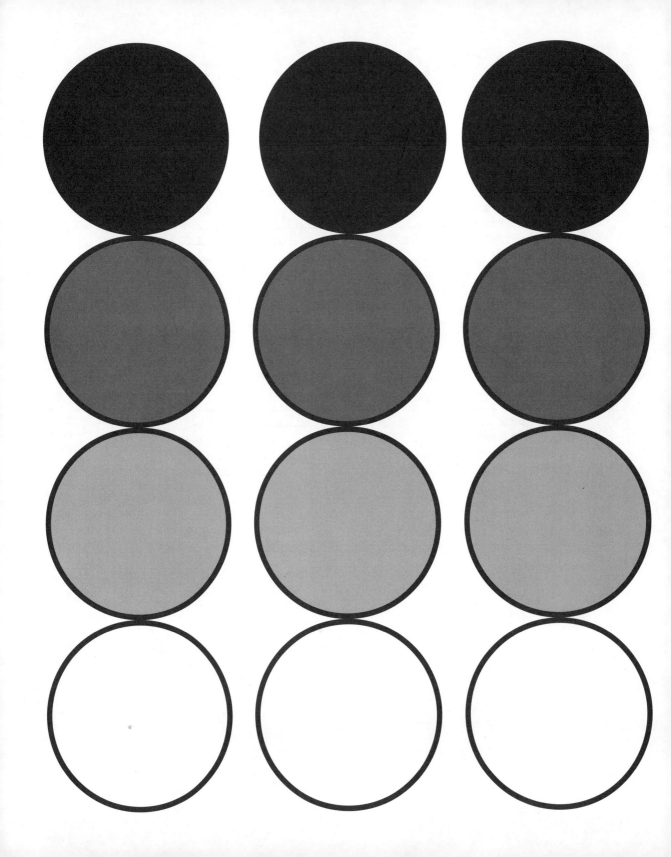

CONCEPTS

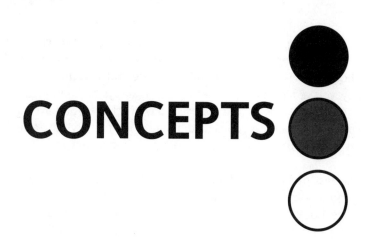

Introduction

If you've got as far as opening up this book, then you've probably got, or are going to get, Photoshop Elements. You certainly have a rough idea what Photoshop can do for you; whether that is to help you organize your digital photo collection, create great web graphics or sneakily airbrush yourself into places you've never been.

What this book is not going to do is to waste your time telling you all that again. There will be no eulogizing about the wonders of Photoshop Elements, fantastic though it is. There will be no discussion about the author's favorite coffee bar (it's probably been turned into a Starbucks anyway), and there will definitely not be any "To my darling Jemima...".

What we are going to do is show you how to do what you want with Photoshop Elements as quickly as possible. This book has been carefully designed to organize information in the most efficient possible manner for a new user, so before you dive in, please take a moment to familiarize yourself with the idea behind it. If you do, you'll be doing in a matter of hours what a traditional book would take days or weeks to teach.

How to Use This Book

Like any computer program these days, Elements is capable of many different tasks, some of which you might never need, others of which you'll probably want to get on with straight away. So, rather than wasting your valuable time, we've taken the opportunity to find the concepts behind Elements and bring them right to the beginning of the book.

This first chapter, which you're already reading, will teach you the basics you need to know and remember in order to use Photoshop. There's nothing difficult here, but if you read it – and hey, you've already started – then you'll always feel comfortable in Photoshop. Think of it as your first day at school; you have to find your way around so you can continue to learn everything else, but no one will try and teach you anything complicated.

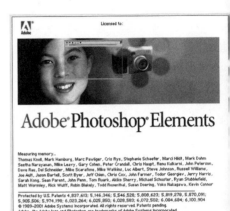

The rest of the book shows you how do things you actually want to do in a manner you can easily adapt to your own work. Unlike some books, this isn't a chance for the author to show you his family photo album. The things we do can easily be applied to your work (or play). Not only that; but because there aren't painstakingly long lessons all over the place, you can dip in anywhere you like, whenever you like. Get a job done by flicking through until you see what you want, or make your way steadily through the book until you know everything that there is to know. It's up to you.

Finally, at the end we've included two pieces of work that you might be interested in. One by a "New Master", an experienced Photoshop user creating real commercial work. The other by another pro-level designer. "Hang on a minute," you say, "I thought you said you weren't going to waste our time with things we couldn't do?" Don't worry – there are step-by-step instructions showing you how it was done. In other words, we're going to show you how Photoshop makes even professional design easy!

Layout Points

Throughout the text you will find references to menu commands. Instead of telling you to "click on the 'File' menu, drag your pointer to the 'Open' and click again", we'll just write File > Open. You'll also occasionally find **Important Words** picked out and, where there's something worth knowing that doesn't really fit into the body of the text, it'll appear in a tip box (don't worry – you'll recognize one as soon as you see one!). Easy, huh?

Support

In addition, we'll provide a number of the files shown within the pages of this book for you to work with if you wish. There's no need to of course, every example is designed to work with your own images, but if you like the download page is at www.friendsofed.com.

You can also e-mail us at support@friendsofed.com, and we will do our best to help you out with any problems you may have. Our e-mails are answered by real people, and we aim to answer you as quickly as possible. Not instantly, like a computer, but usefully and within a few hours or days instead.

Without Further Ado...

We've just promised a quick start and here it is (if you've not yet installed the software now is the time). Welcome to the Photoshop Elements work area. It might look a bit different, depending on whether you're using a Mac or a PC, but you should have no problem locating the basics. If it looks a total mess, click Window > Reset Palette Locations. That should make it look like this screenshot.

Menu Bar   Shortcuts Bar   Options Bar   Palette Well

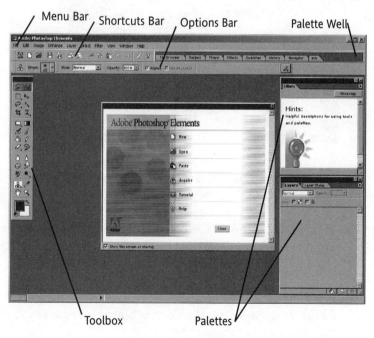

Toolbox   Palettes

The Menu Bar and Shortcuts Bar should be fairly self-explanatory to anyone who's familiar with using a PC. If you need to know more about Menus it's probably best to look at the documentation that came with your computer.

The Shortcuts bar just provides quicker ways of doing all the boring but necessary things like saving files, printing and, of course, undoing mistakes. It is very similar to one you might find in other software packages, like a word processor.

Although the majority of the images in this book are taken from the PC version, Elements also works on the Mac. Everything looks essentially the same, and in this book we've written keyboard shortcuts for both operating systems, PC first:

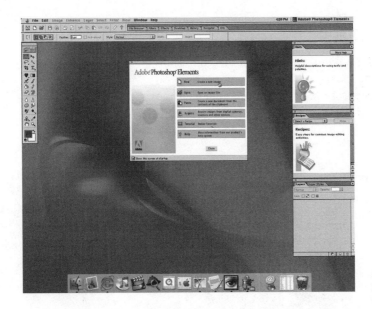

- Ctrl/Z-C: Press Ctrl and C at the same time on a PC, Press Z (Command) and C at the same time on a Mac

- Ctrl/Z-Shift-C: Press Ctrl and Shift and C at the same time on a PC, Press Z (Command) and shift and C at the same time on a Mac

- Right/Ctrl-Click: PC users click with the right button of the mouse, Mac users press the Control button on your keyboard and click with the mouse button.

TIP: Advanced users might benefit from the more complete list of keyboard shortcuts found in Appendix 2.

TIP: Although the demo version does not work in Mac OS X, the full version will run in 'Classic' mode.

Toolbox

The rest may be unfamiliar to anyone who is only used to, for example, Microsoft Word. On the left hand side of the screen (though you can put it where you like) is a Toolbox which contains the main Photoshop tools. For the most part these are the tools which affect the document you are working on, and it allows you to switch between, say, the Airbrush tool or the magnifying glass (Zoom tool).

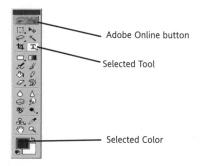

Adobe Online button

Selected Tool

Selected Color

Not all of the tools are shown at once – some are grouped behind a single button, like the Lasso tool

Where there are tools 'hidden' like this, a small triangle at the bottom right of the tool indicates this. Click and hold with the mouse button to reveal the other tools, which are always closely related. The most recently selected one will remain visible on the toolbar.

> TIP: The letter to the right of the tool's name is its keyboard shortcut – you can use these to access the tools too.

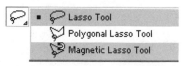

When you select a tool, the Options Bar (below the Shortcut Bar) changes to reflect the tool you have chosen. If, for example, you click on the text tool T, the toolbar will look a bit like one on a word processor, allowing you to change the typeface you are working with. Each tool has its own options bar. Try clicking on a few now but, as we've not opened a file yet, you won't really be able to do anything.

The currently selected tool
(also appears 'pressed' in the Toolbox)

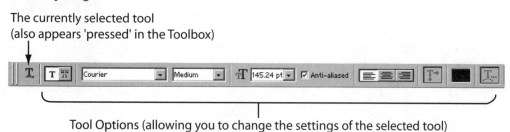

Tool Options (allowing you to change the settings of the selected tool)

Palettes

Photoshop Elements, in common with many popular design and drawing programs, uses little windows, called Palettes, to help the user find the tools they need. They're handy because you can have as many or as few as you like on the screen at once, depending on what you're working on, or the size of your monitor. Real pros often have two monitors connected to the same computer with their palettes on one screen and their work on the other.

Working with palettes takes some getting used to. The key to using them is the little tab where the palette's name is written. Although you can move the palettes around like little windows (they obey the conventions of Windows or MacOS for re-sizing), if you click and drag on the tab you can move the palette behind another, or up into the **Palette Well** (or **Palette Dock**) (the gray box, located to the right of the Shortcut Bar).

Let's start by putting the Hints palette out of the way – it's not very useful and it's taking up valuable space on the screen.

1. Click and drag on the Hints 'tab'.

2. Move the palette to the Palette Well and let go of the mouse.

3. The tab now appears with the others in the well.

You can bring it back whenever you like by dragging it out of the well, or you can use it from the well (dock) by clicking on it once.

Not only is there a Palette Well at the top of the screen, but each individual palette can also act in much the same way. On the default layout, for example, the Layer Styles palette is tucked behind the Layer palette.

TIP: To return to the default palette layout use the menu command Window > Reset Palette Locations.

By clicking once on the tab behind you'll bring it to the front of the palette, in the same way as clicking once on the tab in the Palette Well brought the palette up. Palette tabs can also be clicked and dragged into other palettes – so you could, for example, drag the Layers tab into the Colors palette, or vice versa.

Combining palettes in this way lets you access the functions easily, without having to have several open palettes on the screen. Using these methods, you can arrange your palettes to suit your style of work and the size of your monitor.

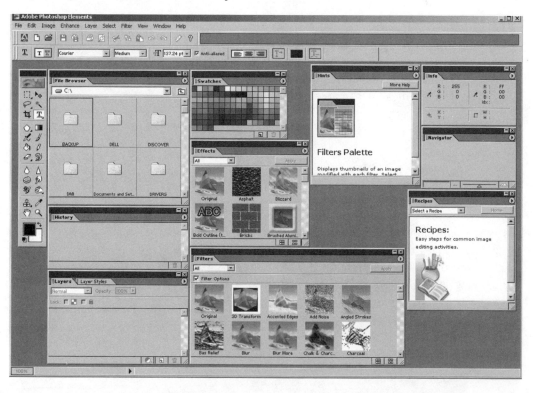

Notice how, when all the palettes are out, that the Palette Well (or dock) appears empty. Of course, it's not a very effective way of working either, as virtually the whole screen is taken up before we've even opened a picture file.

Using Palettes

Aside from the tabs, each palette has two other things in common: a menu button at the top that brings up options (different for each palette) and a button bar at the bottom that varies depending on the functions that the palette carries out. For example, the garbage can icon on the Swatch palette's Button Bar can be used to throw away unnecessary colors by simply clicking on then and dragging them onto the button.

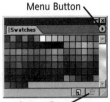

Menu Button

Button Bar

And that's as much as we need to know about the work area for the time being. Once you've got used to the basics it becomes second nature, in the same way as using the button bar at the top of a word processor. At this stage, you might want to take a moment to get familiar with dragging the palettes behind each other and to and from the well.

Preferences

Photoshop Elements also includes a set-up dialogue that allows you to set many options the way you like. When the preferences dialogue is mentioned in the rest of the book, this is the one we mean. It is accessed by clicking Edit > Preferences... > General.

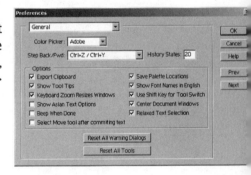

As with many other dialogues in Photoshop, there are a number of pages to the Preferences dialogue accessed by clicking on the pull-down menu at the top of the page, or by clicking on a different option when you open the dialogue (e.g. Edit > Preferences... > Saving Files...). Many of these options are quite self-explanatory, others aren't:

- **General** – Perhaps the most useful option on this page is to adjust the number of History States. If you have a lot of spare memory, you may want to increase the number, if Photoshop is running slowly try decreasing it.

- **Saving Files** – An important point here is the backwards compatibility option. If you are not swapping your files with a user of a early version of Photoshop, then you should uncheck this box.

- **Displays and Cursors** – This section allows you to alter the cursors (mouse pointer) shapes that Photoshop uses. You can choose more accurate ones, or ones that remind you what tool you are using.

- **Transparency** – These settings allow you to adjust the pattern your computer uses to represent transparent regions of an image. This is useful if you find the default (white and grey squares) too close to the colors in your image.

- **Units/Rulers** – This allows you to choose your preferred measurements. Not just traditional centimeters and inches, but Points and Picas (printers measurements) as well.

- **Grid** – Adjust the color/spacing of the Grid (which you can turn on and off when editing an image to help position things).

- **Plugins & Scratch Disks** – These options allow you to tell Photoshop where it can find things. Plugins are additional features that you can by from other software companies. Scratch Disks are the space you PC uses to save History steps when you don't have enough memory. You can make Photoshop faster by placing this on a different Hard Disc to the one where Photoshop is installed.

- **Memory & Image Cache** – Allows you to adjust the amount of physical memory (RAM) Photoshop gobbles up. Don't put it above 50% if you're using other programs at the same time.

A Bit of Theory

If you new to editing images on a computer there are just a few bits of theory that you really ought to know. It may be a little boring, but it's important, simple, and you'll only have to learn it once. Although we're looking at it from a Photoshop perspective, all the theory discussed here is common to many, if not all, similar programs.

Resolution

There are two different ways computers handle images, called bitmap and vector. Vector graphics describe individual lines using points and mathematics so that they can be viewed at any scale without any loss of detail. This is, for example, how your computer stores fonts so that you can print them at different sizes.

Photographs, on the other hand, are traditionally saved as **Bitmap** files, which effectively divide a picture into a grid and record a color for each individual square, or **pixel,** as they are called. This means that when you zoom in on a bitmap image, it becomes **pixelated**, meaning that you can see the pixels as jagged edges. The more different the adjoining colors, the more apparent this is.

This means that you have to ensure the image you take has enough detail in the first place. The traditional measure of this is Dots Per Inch, **dpi**. The dots, in this case, are the pixels, and the inch is measured in a straight line – so for a square inch at 100 dpi there are 100x100 pixels.

So, if an average photo is 6 x 4 inches is stored on your computer at 100dpi, that's 240,000 pixels. At 300dpi that's 2.16 million pixels. Computers are powerful these days, but not fast enough to handle images of indefinite size. Resolution is something you have to keep your eye on. It is a constant trade off between resolution and workability – if it's too low then those jaggy edges will be too apparent, if it's too big your computer will run out of storage space.

If the only place your picture is ever going to be seen is on a computer screen (the web, a handheld, whatever) it's really easy – then it only needs to be 72dpi. Some monitors work at 96dpi, but it's close enough not to make too much difference. This is a recognized standard. For a home or desktop printer, 150dpi is perfectly acceptable.

Your printer will no doubt claim a far higher resolution – something like 1440dpi or even more than that – but that's a slightly different measure as it's talking about the dots of ink it uses to represent other colors. Desktop printers use three, four or six colors and mix them in patterns of tiny dots to represent the many millions of colors computer pixels are capable of being set at.

Warsaw Palace of Culture scanned at 50dpi   and at 300dpi

We've already learnt more about printing technology than we'd like, so this next comment is going to be really refreshing: For professional printing (magazine pictures, for example) the best solution is to, well, ask the printer what they'd like. No odd rules, nothing to remember. Don't worry – they'll be nice – you're paying them!

> TIP: dpi (dots per inch) is often used interchangeably with the more accurate ppi (pixels per inch).

Viewing Resolution

Changing the resolution does not in any way affect the number of pixels in an image. What it does do is tell the computer what size on a printed page the pixels should be. In other words, how big your picture is. The best way to get the hang of this concept is to try it out.

1. Open a picture file of some sort. If you have a scanner, scan one of your own at 200dpi. If you really can't find anything, there is a picture of Oslo Royal Palace, Norway on the Friends of ED web site, where you'll find the other support files for this book. http://www.friendsofed.com.

2. Click on the Zoom tool (indicated by the magnifying glass), and notice that the Options bar at the top changes to reveal, among other things buttons marked 'Actual Pixels' and 'Print Size'.

3. Click on them and you should find that the picture changes size. When you click on Actual Pixels the image shows every individual pixel in the image in one pixel of your monitor (which is either 72 or 96 dpi).

> TIP: If you have a Scanner, Photoshop will allow you to use it by clicking File > Import > Name of Your Scanner.

4. When you click on the **Print Size** button, the image changes size to reflect the size the image would appear if printed. In doing this the computer will use the dpi setting it has recorded for your monitor – this might not be an inch-perfect representation of the final print size, but it is usually fairly accurate.

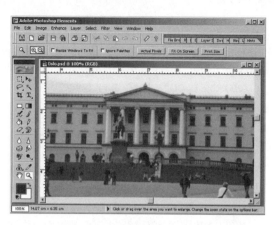

Changing the Resolution

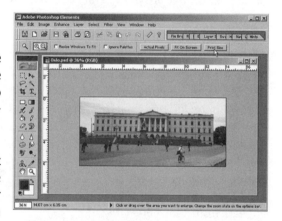

1. If the two images are the same size then the picture's resolution is the same as that of your monitor. To change the resolution click Image > Resize > Image Size...

2. Uncheck the Resample Image box at the bottom. If you change the size with this box checked, the computer will adjust the number of pixels in each direction and leave the resolution the same (which can be problematic, for reasons explained below).

3. Type a new figure in the Resolution box – set it at half the previous size (here I've set it from 200dpi to 100dpi).

4. Click OK.

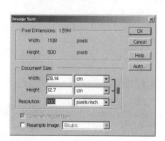

Now, when you select the Zoom tool and the Print Size button you'll see that the image will print twice as large on the page. There's the same amount of information (pixels) there, but spread over twice the area.

Except for professional level work, resolution can often be sidestepped. For example, if you import an image into Microsoft Word (or many other Word Processors, it is not fixed at a certain size, but can be re-sized in much the same way as in Photoshop. Indeed Photoshop itself allows you to re-size images at the printing stage without affecting the size and resolution you have been working on (details on this are in the Output chapter).

> TIP: With a digital camera the resolution will be determined when you take the photo – it's best to check your camera's settings, as you can't re-scan the snap!

Changing the Number of Pixels (Size)

There is just one rule here – don't increase the number of pixels. To make the image larger, either adjust the resolution, or scale it up in a word-processor later. The reason is simple; Photoshop can't make information appear from nowhere. It's very tempting to try to make this image of the Prague skyline more detailed by increasing the size, but it is fruitless.

This image is the smaller image increased in size.

This image is scanned at a higher resolution and is not zoomed.

Scaling images the other way is perfectly acceptable if you find that you have more detail than you need. To do it we use the same dialogue as before:

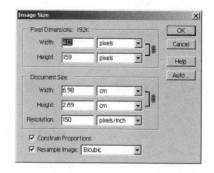

1. Click Image > Resize > Image Size...

2. In the dialogue that appears, change the width value to a lower one. If you want to make the image half size, click on the pull down menu to the right of the box marked 'pixels' and choose percent. Then put '50' in the pixel Width box. The Resample Image checkbox needs to be checked in order to adjust pixel dimensions.

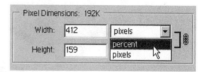

3. Click OK. Your picture will now be half size (a quarter of the number of pixels).

TIP: You can adjust any of the values in the box in order to adjust the size of the picture.

Color Theory

We've just seen that the image is composed of pixels, each of which is set at a certain color. Computers describe color in terms of Red, Green and Blue, which mix to produce white (this is called **additive** color) whereas your printer starts with white (paper) and adds cyan (blue), magenta (red), and yellow to get away from white (**subtractive** color).

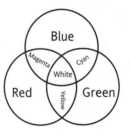

When we see colors in the real world, we see a little more than this – all the colors in the rainbow in fact. You can see this yourself by looking at light through a prism or, depending on the weather, by waiting for a Rainbow (which is the effect of viewing sunlight though rain, each rain droplet acting as a prism).

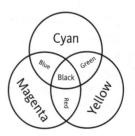

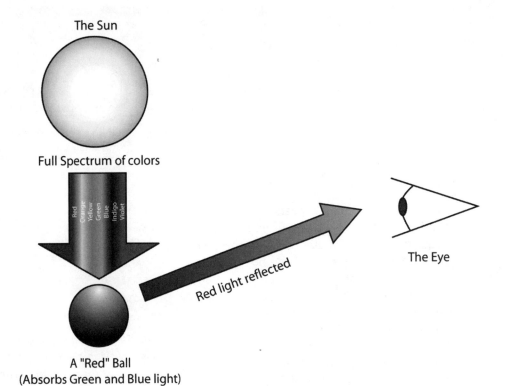

The Sun

Full Spectrum of colors

Red Orange Yellow Green Blue Indigo Violet

Red light reflected

The Eye

A "Red" Ball
(Absorbs Green and Blue light)

The computer cheats a little, by selecting just three of the colors – Red, Green and Blue, but they mix to produce nearly every color under the sun. Each color is assigned a value between zero and 255 (256 possible shades). Multiplying the three gives a total of 16.8 million colors, also known as 24-bit color. It is possible for your computer to record even higher numbers of shades (say 48-bit color) but the differences are rarely visible on your computer screen.

As a set of **Primary Colors**, Red, Green and Blue (RGB) can actually represent a greater range of tones (known as a **gamut**) than CMY. Many color printers help compensate for this by using an extra black (known as key) ink, but even then your desktop printer will never be able to perfectly match all the hues that can appear on your monitor.

Red	Green	Blue	
255	+ 255	+ 255	= □
0	+ 0	+ 0	= ■

To help compensate for this, Photoshop has color correction facilities, accessed by clicking Edit > Color Settings.... For the most part it is best to leave this set to 'No color management', but if you know your printer has an International Color Consortium color profile then you can turn it on.

File Formats

Just like other applications on your computer, Photoshop Elements loads and saves a variety of file formats. Over the years various different bitmap image file formats have become popular. There are many others, and if you need to use them you no doubt know about them already, but a few are especially important and worth a bit of a look.

> TIP: If you are experiencing problems with color reproduction, try turning this feature off again. It may interfere with your printer drivers.

Photoshop (PSD)

By default Photoshop saves its own file format PSD files. The principle advantage of using this format is that you can continue editing using all the features of Photoshop. Text you've written will remain editable, and layers you create will still be visible. This is sometimes called unflattened. The problem is that they are not universally recognized by other applications, and can be very large files.

Others

Using the File > Save As... dialogue and clicking, you can bring up a long list of other file types to save to. These include:

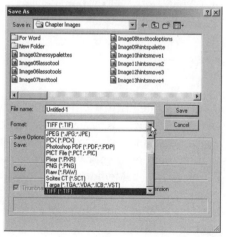

- **TIFF** files save the entire image, and can be read by many different programs, and are especially used by publishers because they are lossless. That means that they save every pixel individually, resulting in a large file size.

- **JPEG** files, on the other hand throw away a lot of information to reduce the file size (this is known as compression). They are handy for sharing on the Internet – either by e-mail or on the web. When you click Save, you are presented with a quality slider. It allows you to adjust the compromise between quality and file size.

These images are cropped from a larger shot of Copenhagen, from the left they are 40k (low), 79k (medium), 224k (high) and the TIFF on the right is 1036k.

Digital Cameras

If you installed software onto your computer when you got your digital camera, Photoshop Elements may well recognize it automatically – you can check by clicking File > Import > and if you see the name of your digital camera software then click on it and Photoshop will automatically download pictures.

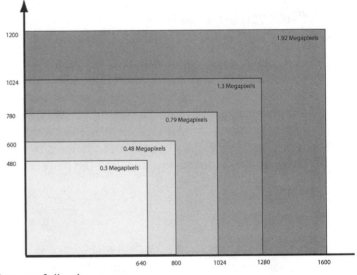

If not, you need to transfer your images following your cameras instructions. Many digital cameras save JPEG files, which you can load into Photoshop in the normal way. Getting them onto your PC might require a cable, or your PC may have a Memory Stick or Compact Flash reader built in. The exact method varies from machine to machine, and you are better placed than us to know what your set up is!

TIP: To ensure the quality of you images, it is worth checking that your camera is set to the largest and highest quality settings. Many cameras can take advantage of extra memory.

If you're planning on buying a digital camera, the most obvious trade off is between price and resolution. In this context resolution means the maximum size of the picture that the camera will take. Typically these equate with traditional PC monitor resolutions, though in sales-speak this gets turned into millions of pixels.

Opening Saved Images

To open a file, regardless of its file format, you can use the File Browser palette. Most images that you can open will be displayed in small (Thumbnail) form.

1. Click once on the File Browser palette tab in the Palette Well.

2. The browser window works much like ordinary windows on your computer. Click on the down arrow to bring up a list of the storage devices where your image file might be.

3. Photoshop will display thumbnails or sub-folders. Double-clicking on a sub folder will move into that folder, double-clicking on an image will open the image for working on.

Photoshop Elements

We've seen the workspace, we've looked at the theory, and now it's nearly time to get stuck in. The last thing that we're going to have a look at is a few essentials of image editing. How to do these things is covered later, but it's just worth mentioning them at this point to give you an idea of how to combine them. If you already know about gamma correction, selection, layers and filters, then carry straight on to whichever chapter interests you.

Enhance

One of the simplest and most effective things you can do to an image is to brighten it up a little, or increase the contrast. Photoshop has some built in facilities to do this which, in some cases, might be all you need to do to bring a muddy picture to life.

Select

You can apply almost any effect to a given region of the image rather than the whole in much the same way as you can make some text bold in a word processor. Selecting areas of an image is not quite as straightforward, so Photoshop includes a number of tools that help you do that.

You can select different parts of the photo at once, and you can **feather** the edges to help the selected effect blend in with the rest of your work.

Layer

Layers enable you to build up an image in much the same way as an animator might use layers of acetate. A good example is the picture of the toolbar we've just seen, where the selection tools have been highlighted. If we could separate the layers and view them from the side, they might look something like this:

- A 'Background' layer with the original picture of the toolbar. Photoshop will always call a new picture a background, though there is nothing to stop you changing the layer order to suit your purposes.

- A black layer with a 'hole' cut into it. We can see through the hole to the original image, but the black blocks it. This whole layer has been made slightly transparent so you can still see underneath, but not as well.

This is just the start – Photoshop allows the use of hundreds of layers. It will also allow you to apply effects to each layer, like shadows or glows. The possibilities are virtually endless, but the real advantage is that layers are quite an easy way to achieve complicated effects and allow you to return to edit beneath them.

Filter

Filters are a way of applying an effect to a whole (or a selected part of) an image, in much the same way that traditional photographers placed filters over the lens. In Photoshop you can achieve traditional effects, like blurs to soften the image, but because the process is mathematical you can also do things that you could never do with a real filter, like mimicking artistic effects.

You can also combine the effects by using them one after the other, which leads us nicely on to the final point of this chapter...

Less is More

This book covers a huge range of exciting features and graphics in Photoshop Elements but that doesn't mean you have to use them every time. It may seem an obvious point, but remember not to get carried away. In many ways the difference between a professional designer and complete novice is that the pro knows when to stop.

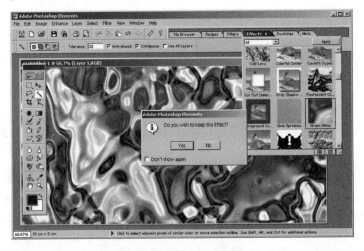

The trick is to keep in mind the result you want to achieve (restoring a damaged print, for example). By all means experiment with the assorted effects – the green slime, for example – but remember that it isn't always appropriate in family photos. Well, not in every family.

It's also worth remembering that there is no need to read every chapter in order if you don't want to. If all you want to do right now is remove dust marks from a photo, by all means skip ahead to Chapter 6. You can always return and work through the other chapters to expand your knowledge at a later date.

And now, with those notes of caution aside, happy Photoshopping...

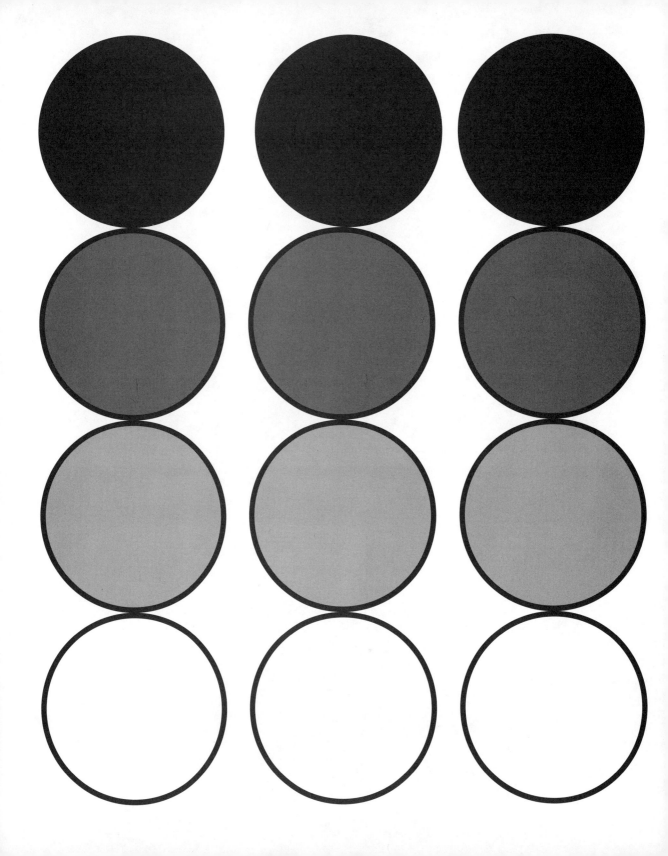

CHAPTER 1
PAINTING

Selecting a Color

Whatever you are planning to do to an image, whether it's adding 'paint' or deleting an area, color is involved. It really helps to pay close attention to your current colors; using black type on a night sky does not lend itself to easy reading!

- Foreground color is applied when you use the Type tool, fill an area, or draw on the canvas.

- Background color is applied when you delete, erase or move anything on the background layer. The area that is exposed is automatically filled with the current background color.

The current foreground and background colors are shown on the toolbar.

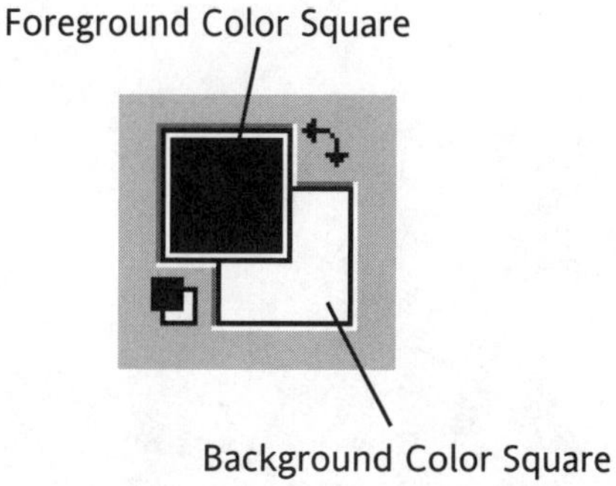

Foreground Color Square

Background Color Square

Switching Between Colors

There are quite a few ways to change your current colors; by entering specific values, picking or sliding to a color in the palette, clicking a pre-chosen swatch or plucking a color from an image using the Eyedropper tool.

To quickly swap your foreground and background color, click the switch icon (the double-headed arrow at the top right of the color indicator).

The icon at the bottom left changes the colors back to their default (black for the foreground and white at the back).

Choosing a Color from the Color Picker

1. To launch the palette click on the foreground or background color square in the Toolbox (whichever you want to change).

Swap Foreground/Background switch

Default (Black/White) switch

TIP: This logo means the color is not guaranteed to display accurately on a website. Click to 'snap' the color to one that will. This will cause the icon to disappear. Alternatively check the 'only web colors' box to limit the selection of colors to ensure web safety.

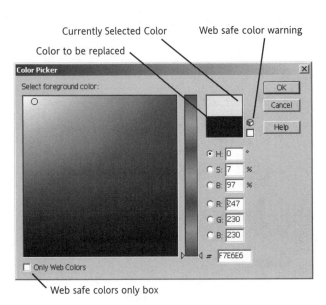

Currently Selected Color

Color to be replaced

Web safe color warning

Web safe colors only box

2. Click somewhere on the Color Slider (the rainbow). The square area will change to reflect the **Hue** you have selected.

3. Now click anywhere in the square to select your final color (which will be shown in your Currently Selected Color box towards the top right of the window).

4. Click OK.

Using Swatches and Saving Color to them

By using the swatches you can create and save custom palettes for each of your projects. The colors crucial to your work will then never get lost.

To select a color, simply click on it to make it the current foreground color.

Saving a Color to the Swatch

1. Click on the foreground color button.

2. Use the color picker as described above to select a color you like.

3. Click on the Add Foreground Color button at the bottom of the swatch, and your square will be added.

4. Repeat the process to add as many colors as you like. You can also remove colors by dragging them from the swatch to the bin in the bottom right hand corner of the palette.

5. Once you're happy with your palette, click on the menu button (top right) and select Save Swatches....

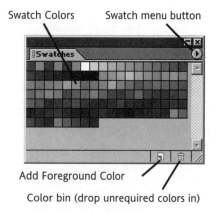

Swatch Colors   Swatch menu button

Add Foreground Color

Color bin (drop unrequired colors in)

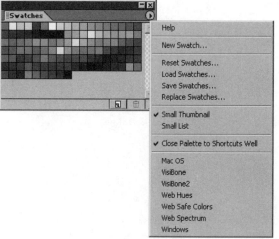

6. Once you give the palette a name and click Save. Photoshop will make your palette available on the palette menu in future.

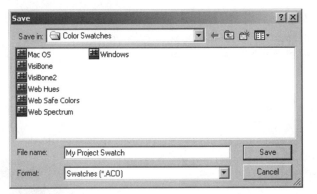

The Eyedropper Tool

You can also use the Eyedropper tool to select a color from anywhere on any image you have open.

1. Select the Eyedropper tool from the Toolbox.

2. Click on the color you want from the image.

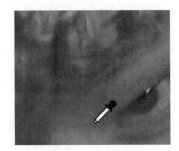

3. If you have trouble getting the color just right, you can select the 'average' color from the pixels neighboring the one you click on by altering the sample area using the Tool Options bar.

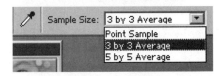

> TIP: If you keep the mouse button held down as you move the Eyedropper tool over your image, the color you are about to select will appear in the foreground color box.

Filling Color

If you need to cover an area with flat color or a gradient, using the Fill tools will save you a lot of time. The main tool is the Paint Bucket, although you should note that this tool can only be used on bitmap images.

Using the Paint Bucket Tool

This tool will fill an area with the foreground color in one click. The area can be confined using the Select tools (see Chapter 2), or will fill the whole canvas on a blank layer.

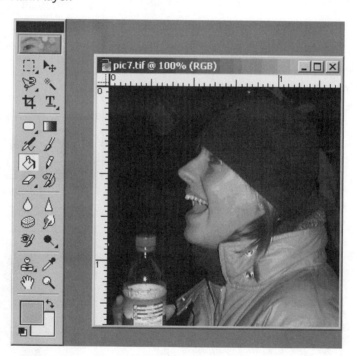

1. Select the Paint Bucket tool.

Fill Bucket tool options bar

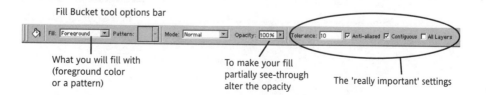

What you will fill with (foreground color or a pattern)

To make your fill partially see-through alter the opacity

The 'really important' settings

2. To fill with the foreground color, ensure that Foreground is selected in the Fill box (to the left), and that the Mode is set to Normal on the Tool Options Bar.

3. The settings at the right hand end can make a significant difference:

- At zero **Tolerance**, the computer only fills colors exactly the same as the one where you click the paint bucket. Its maximum value is 255, which would fill every color.

- Anti-aliasing softens the edge of the filled area.

- Checking the **Contiguous** box means that the computer will only fill around the point where you clicked until the tolerance has been reached. If unchecked, any similar color anywhere in the image can be affected.

- If you're using layers, checking All Layers means that the fill will apply to every layer of the image rather than just the one you're working on.

Original

Filled at 10 Tolerance

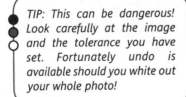

TIP: This can be dangerous! Look carefully at the image and the tolerance you have set. Fortunately undo is available should you white out your whole photo!

Filled at 30 Tolerance

Quickly Using the Gradient Tool

1. Set your foreground and background colors – these become the start and end colors.

2. Select the Gradient tool.

3. Click and drag across the image, marking the start and end points of the gradient color.

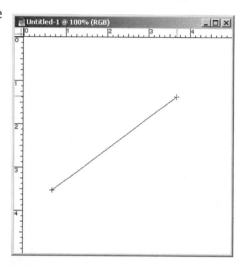

4. When you release the mouse button at the end of the line, a gradient will be drawn, the foreground at the beginning and the background color at the end.

TIP: to constrain a gradient to a certain part of the image, select the fill area using the tools explained in Chapter 2.

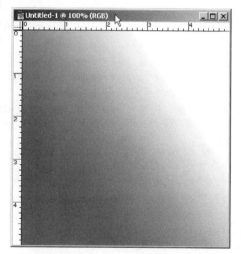

More Complicated Gradients

You don't just have to produce gradients in just in a linear way. In the options try using a radial, angle or diamond fill. You can also use more than just two colors.

1. Select the Gradient tool as before.

2. On the Tool Options bar, click on the Edit button (the button to the right of the example box brings up some presets).

3. On the main horizontal bar the top markers (called opacity stops) control the opacity and the lower markers (called color stops) the color. Double-click on the far left color stop.

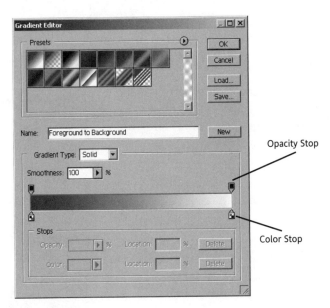

4. A color picker will appear. Select a nice blue (or whatever you feel like) and click OK.

5. Now click somewhere between the two color markers at the bottom. A new color point will appear.

6. Click on the color below and select a color for this marker – we've gone for bright red.

7. Now click on and drag the color midpoint marker on the left, nearer to our new centre color point.

8. Click OK to set the gradient and return to the canvas.

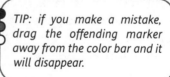

TIP: *if you make a mistake, drag the offending marker away from the color bar and it will disappear.*

9. Using the Tool Options bar, select radial gradient (or any other style that suits you).

10. Click and drag from near the centre of your image to some way out.

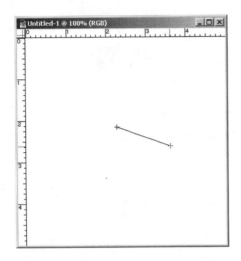 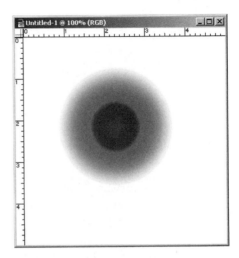

The result is a gradation with more than one tone, and different blending. As the psychedelic presets show, there are plenty of possibilities here.

Brushes

Like the Fill tools, the brushes are used to 'enhance' an image, but are controlled more directly by the user. Here we'll look at the more traditional tools; the Paintbrush and the Airbrush.

The Paintbrush paints thick opaque paint, no matter how many times you paint over the area. Changing the opacity in the options will give a consistent translucent coverage.

The option of wet edges for the Paintbrush gives the illusion that the canvas is wet. The example shows a normal stroke and then with the wet edges box checked.

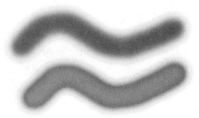

1. Open a new image to work with.

2. Select the Paintbrush tool.

3. Using the Tool Options bar, select a brush size and shape you like.

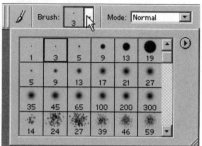

4. At the right end of the Tool Options bar, the brush dynamics dropdown allows you to set fade options, which are measured in steps, each step equaling a brush mark:

   ● Size – the brush decreases in size towards the end of your stroke.

   ● Opacity – the brush fades to transparent as you draw across the page.

   ● Color – the brush will fade from the foreground to background color over the length of your stroke.

5. Click where you want your stroke to start and drag it across the page. If you've set a fade option it may stop itself. If not, it will stop as soon as you release the mouse button.

The Airbrush

Like the real thing, the Airbrush is much more sensitive than the Paintbrush. Set the pressure in the options to 100% and it will appear thick like the paintbrush. At 10% it paints lightly, but the more you hover over an area the more saturated it will become.

a stroke of the paintbrush

the same stroke with an
airbrush at 10%

Changing Brushes

In the last example I used a round brush, but as before there are quite a few brush tips available, from soft edges to small paint splatters that look like footprints. Click the tip preview in the brush options and choose a brush that best suits your needs.

Modifying Existing Brushes

1. Click on the brush tip preview to open the brush options.

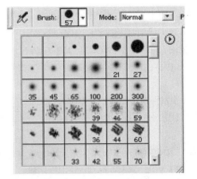

2. Click on the menu button at the top left of the brush options box and select New Brush... from the resulting menu.

3. Move the diameter slider to make the brush larger or smaller.

4. The Hardness option set towards the left makes the edges softer.

5. Move the Spacing slider to the right to have the brush just leave marks at regular intervals on the canvas. You can switch off Spacing entirely by unchecking the Spacing box, so that the line you draw will be continuous.

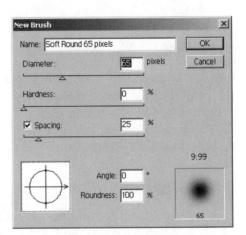

6. Change the roundness to 50% and the angle to 60 and the brush would look like this:

Custom Brushes

To use your image as a brush tip, select the area of the image you want to use and choose Edit > Define Brush. Enter a name and the new brush will appear with those available.

Using the Brush Blending Modes

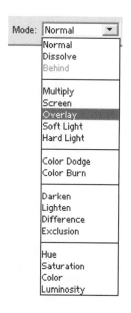

The blend mode controls how the color you are applying affects the underlying image. This results in a blend color.

Choose the blend mode before you apply the stroke. The mode can be selected from the options.

In the following examples I've applied a dark (left) and a light color (right) so you can see the result at a glance. The results are best viewed in color though, so can be downloaded from our website at www.friendsofed.com.

Normal: Each pixel you paint becomes the blend color, overwriting underlying pixels.

Dissolve: is the same as the normal mode, but with a random placement of pixels. Saturation of the placement depends on the opacity of the brush. Works best with a large brush.

Multiply: Multiplies the applied color with the underlying color, so that the darkest (strongest) color remains.

Screen: The same as multiply but with the inverse of the two values, so that lighter brushes have more effect.

Overlay: The underlying color is mixed with the applied color and reflects the lightness or darkness of the original image

Softlight: Darkens or lightens the image depending on the applied color. The result is muted.

Hardlight: Darkens or lightens the image depending on the applied color. The result is harsh.

Color Dodge: Brightens the base color to reflect the applied color.

Color Burn: Darkens the base color to reflect the applied color.

Darken: Selects the darkest color (the brush color or the image below) and applies that.

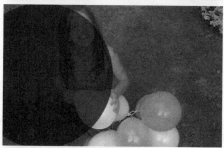

Lighten: Selects the lightest color and uses that as the blend color.

Difference: Creates a photographic negative effect. The lighter the color the more pronounced the result, so black has no effect.

Exclusion: Produces a similar effect to the difference mode but with less contrast.

Hue: Creates a result color with the luminosity and saturation of the base color and the hue of the blend color.

Saturation: Creates a result color with the luminosity and hue of the base color and the saturation of the blend color.

Color: Creates a result color with the luminosity of the base color and the hue and saturation of the blend color. Good for tinting images.

Luminosity: Creates a result color with the hue and saturation of the base color and the luminosity of the blend color. The result is inverse to the color mode.

Using History

In addition to the undo button common to the majority of media applications, Photoshop saves up to 99 previous states of undo. They are saved in the History palette. It displays the most recent state applied to an image from the bottom up. Clicking on a prior state restores the image to that stage in your work history.

> TIP: To change the number of states Photoshop records, enter the number (1-100) in the History States box in the general preferences under the Edit menu. When you exceed this number the earliest states will be written over.

The history only memorizes states from your current session. If you reopen a previous project you will find the history blank.

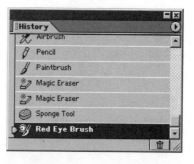

Using the History Palette

1. If you wish to undo several previous steps while working on an image, then click on a previous point. The one you click on will be the last thing you did to still appear in the image.

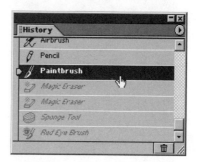

2. You can still return to the 'greyed out' (more recent) steps below by clicking on them.

3. As soon as you use another tool (the Gradient tool here), all the actions below the currently selected one will disappear and will not become available again should you click undo (the Undo tool will use the 'new' history).

4. If, for any reason, you want to delete the previous states, drag a past state to the bin in the bottom right hand corner of the palette and all states prior to that one will be removed.

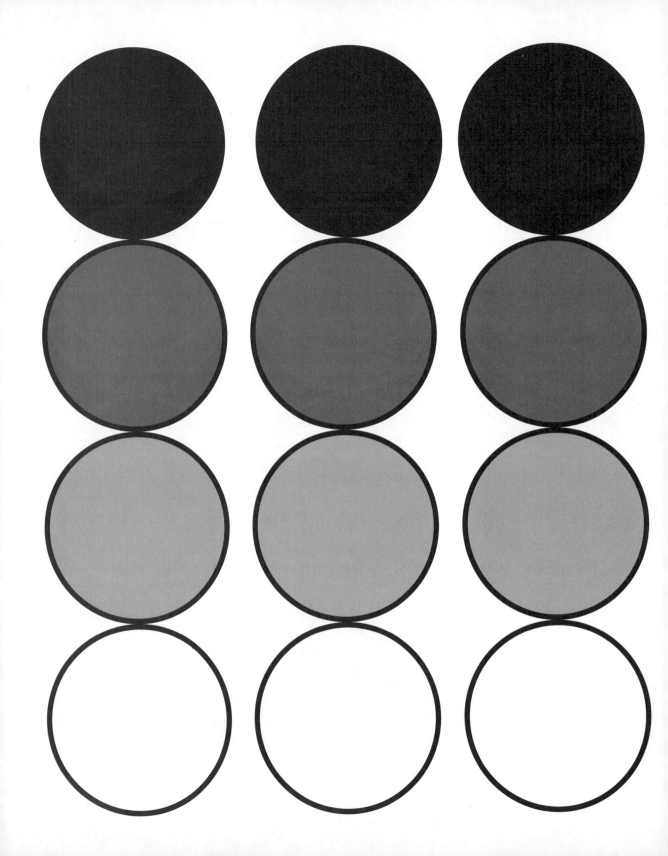

CHAPTER 2
SELECTION

Photoshop is a bitmap program, meaning that Photoshop images are not made up of objects but of pixels. Selection is very important in Photoshop, because if we want to change a single part of an image we have to select it. If, for example, we are working on an image of a tree in a landscape, Photoshop cannot automatically tell the difference between the tree and the rest of the picture, it just sees an arrangement of differently colored pixels. So, to make changes only to the tree, and not the rest of the image, we need to select the pixels that make up the tree.

Photoshop has a number of tools that enable selection: the Rectangular Marquee tool, the Elliptical Marquee Tool, the Lasso Tool, the Polygonal Lasso tool, the Magnetic Lasso tool and the Magic Wand tool. All these tools do essentially the same thing – select pixels. Depending on the kind of image that we are working on, or how accurate the selection needs to be, certain tools are better than others.

The Selection tools work by drawing marquees. Marquees are flashing black and white lines (also called 'marching ants') that indicate boundaries between selected pixels and unselected pixels (the pixels inside the marquee are the selected pixels). When a marquee has been made, only the pixels inside the marquee can be changed. This is why selection is so essential to users of Photoshop, because it allows us to make changes (such as adjusting the color, changing the scale or applying effects) to specific parts of our images, without changing the rest of the image.

This chapter will introduce and explain the merits and the uses of each of the Selection tools as well as how they can be modified to suit our needs. At the end of the chapter there is a page of shortcuts that will help save time when working with selections, once you are familiar with the tools.

Basic Selections

The Rectangular and Elliptical Marquee tools (as their names suggest) allow you to make rectangular and elliptical selections. This is useful when making quick, rough selections or selections that need to be geometric.

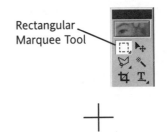

Rectangular Marquee Tool

Rectangular Selections

To select a rectangle or square of pixels in your image, select the Rectangular Marquee tool in the Toolbox.

Move the cursor over your image. Notice that the cursor changes into a cross.

Make a selection by clicking and dragging the cursor over part of the image. When you let go of the mouse you will see a box made of moving black and white lines. This is your **Marquee**. The pixels inside the Marquee are selected. The point where you clicked is one corner of the marquee, and where you stopped dragging (or released the mouse) is the opposite corner.

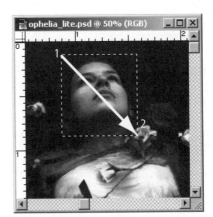

TIP: If you prefer to draw a rectangle or an ellipse from the center, click and hold the Alt key while you drag. This allows you to stretch the shape from the center until you are satisfied with the shape.

Elliptical Selections

To make an **Elliptical selection**, go back to the Toolbox and leave the mouse pressed down on the Rectangular marquee tool, until a box with more related tools appears (you can also use 'Shift-M' to access this).

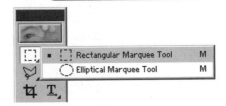

Click on the Elliptical Marquee tool and notice that the icon in your Toolbox has changed from a square to a circle. It is now possible to make elliptical selections.

Click and drag the cursor across part of your image. When you let go of the mouse there will be a circle made up of flashing black and white lines (an elliptical marquee) showing the elliptical area of pixels that have been selected.

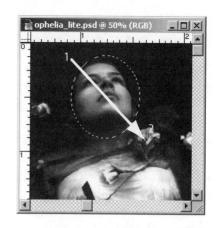

Deselecting

To deselect, do so by either:

- Pressing Ctrl/⌘-D on your keyboard.

- Going to the **Select** menu and then **Deselect**.

- Clicking anywhere on the screen, outside the selected area.

The Marquee Tool Options Bar

When a Marquee Tool is selected, the Tool Options Bar changes to offer a number of options that allow you to modify your selections. It allows you to add to your selections, subtract from your selections, make new selections, feather your selection, ask for an anti-aliased selection and change the style of your selection. These, and additional options, can also be accessed via keyboard shortcuts (see the list at the end of this chapter) and via the Select menu.

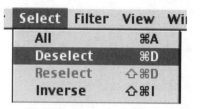

TIP: It is important to deselect after working in the selected area because, until you have deselected, all the pixels outside of the marquee remain inactive. If, after you have made selections, you find that you are unable to work on the image, it is probably because a very small selection has accidentally been made.

TIP: Check Anti-aliasing to prevent jagged lines when making selections

Creating & Amending Selections.

On the left-hand side of the Marquee Status bar you will see four small icons. By clicking on the different icons you can create new, add to, subtract from and intersect selections.

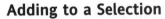

—— Intersect with an existing selection
—— Subtract from an existing selection
—— Add to an exisiting selection
—— Create a new selection

Making a New Selection

With the **new selection** icon pressed down (the default icon) the cursor changes to a cross as it moves over the image. Select an area of your image. Now make another selection. Notice that the first selection disappears – every time you click and drag the cursor across part of the image, a new selection replaces the last.

Adding to a Selection

Now press the **Add to selection** icon in the status bar. As you move the cursor across your image you will see that the cross icon now has a little + sign next to it.

Try making a number of selections over your image.   Change to a different marquee between selections if you like.

Notice that there are now a number of marquees on the image – the pixels inside each of the marquees are now selected.

Add to the shape of an existing selection by clicking and dragging a rectangular marquee over one of the existing selections.

Subtracting From a Selection

Select the **Subtract icon** in the status bar. The icon changes to a cross with a – sign next to it.

Drag a marquee inside an existing selection. Now the area inside the new marquee has been deselected (your original selection has a hole in it).

Cut into the side of a selection by making a marquee that is half in, half out of an existing selection

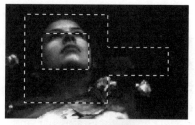

Intersecting Selections

Select the Intersect icon in the status bar. The icon changes to a cross with a x sign next to it.

Drag a marquee over part of two or more of your existing selections. This eliminates the parts of the former selections that are outside of the new marquee. Try it out several times, and watch what happens so that you understand how this tool works

Feathering Selections

Feathering softens the edge of a selection; it gives a smooth transition between the selected pixels and the non-selected pixels. In the options bar you will see a box next to **Feather**.

Feather: 10 px   ☐ Anti-aliased

This allows you to input how many pixels you want the feather to be. If you want the feather to be small (for transition between selected and non-selected pixels to be sharp), or if the resolution of your image is low, put in a low value. If you want the feather to be large (for the transition between selected and non-selected pixels to be more gradual) or if the resolution of your image is high, put in a higher value.

No feather   10 pixel feather   20 pixel feather

Making Selections With a Constrained Aspect Ratio

For symmetrical selections (if you want rectangles to be perfect squares or ellipses to be perfect circles) go to the Status bar and click on the drop-down menu next to **Style**.

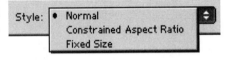

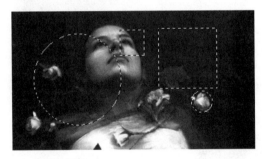

TIP: Another way to ensure that your geometric selections are symmetrical is to click and drag as normal, then press and hold Shift before you release the mouse button.

Select **Constrained Aspect Ratio**. All the marquees that you now make with this option selected will be symmetrical.

Making Selections of a Fixed Size

In the drop-down menu next to **Style** select **Fixed Size**. The boxes to the right of the menu will become active. Enter values into the height and width boxes (the values have to be smaller than the size of your image, otherwise the whole of the image will be selected).

When you click on the image a marquee with the specified dimensions is made (Photoshop takes the place where the mouse is clicked as the top right hand corner of the selection).

100px by 100px   50px by 100px   200px by 100px

Freehand Selections

The Lasso, Polygonal Lasso, and Magnetic lasso tools are for making freehand (user-defined) selections. The Lasso allows basic freehand selections; the Polygonal Lasso allows freehand selections with straight edges, and the Magnetic Lasso follows the edges of objects in your image.

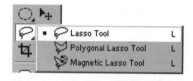

The Lasso

Select the Lasso tool from the Toolbox. Make a freehand selection on your image by clicking and dragging around an area of your image. Photoshop closes the selection by joining the start point to the end point with a straight line. Try to make your end point the same as your start point.

Photoshop joins the start point with the end point with a straight line.

Here the start point and the end point are in the same place.

Notice that the status bar has changed.

There are options to add to, subtract from, and intersect existing selections. It is also possible to ask for feathered and anti-aliased selections. These options work in exactly same way as they did with the Rectangular and Elliptical Marquee tools that we looked at earlier in the chapter. The add-to, and subtract-from modes of this tool are very useful, as it is often tricky to get your desired shape for a marquee first time.

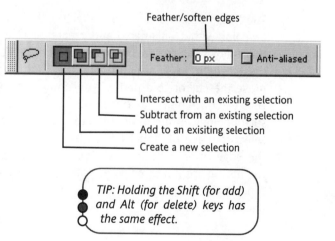

Feather/soften edges

Intersect with an existing selection
Subtract from an existing selection
Add to an exisiting selection
Create a new selection

TIP: Holding the Shift (for add) and Alt (for delete) keys has the same effect.

The Polygonal Lasso

Select the Polygonal Lasso tool (it is hidden behind the Lasso tool. To find it keep the mouse down over the Lasso and select it from the menu that appears).

Click anywhere on your image once, move to another part of the image and click again. A flashing black and white line appears. Move the mouse again and click. Keep doing this until you have created your desired shape. To close the shape either click on the start point or double-click the mouse (in which case Photoshop will close the selection with a straight line from the end point to the start point). When you are close to closing the selection a small circle will appear next to the Lasso icon.

This tool is a bit like sticky bubble gum and can often create lines everywhere if you are a bit too click-happy. This tool can be very useful however if you go slowly and be sure of where you are clicking.

As with the regular Lasso, it is also possible to add to, subtract from and intersect existing selections, as well as feather and anti-alias selections, via the Tool Options Bar, or by using keyboard shortcuts

The Magnetic Lasso Tool

The Magnetic Lasso works by detecting the contrast of color within an image, and creates a selection that follows the changes in color in an image. To use the Magnetic Lasso select it from the Tool box and move the cursor to a part of your image you want to select that is a different color from its surroundings. In the example here I have chosen to select the face of Ophelia. Start by clicking once at the edge of your desired selection and then guide the mouse around its edge. As you move the mouse around the shape Photoshop deposits a line with anchor points.

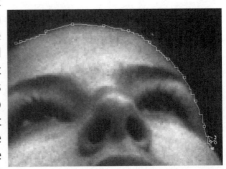

Keep guiding the mouse around the shape until it meets the start point and closes, leaving you with a contrast-defined selection. If, when the Magic wand is laying down points it places one in a place that you don't want or feel is misplaced, press delete or backspace on your keyboard, while pressing the mouse button.

The Magnetic tool status bar allows you to decide how sensitive the tool is, how many anchor points it deposits and width of the area that it searches for color changes.

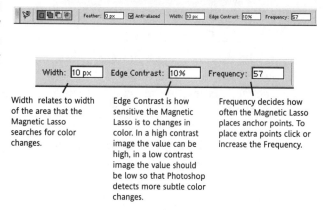

Width relates to width of the area that the Magnetic Lasso searches for color changes.

Edge Contrast is how sensitive the Magnetic Lasso is to changes in color. In a high contrast image the value can be high, in a low contrast image the value should be low so that Photoshop detects more subtle color changes.

Frequency decides how often the Magnetic Lasso places anchor points. To place extra points click or increase the Frequency.

Magic Wand Selection

The Magic Wand tool makes selections based on color similarity. It selects an area of pixels that are similar in color to the pixel that is clicked on. The range of colors that the Magic Wand will select as similar to the chosen pixel is decided by the **Tolerance**. Tolerance can be changed in the Magic Wand status bar.

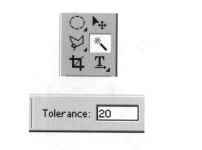

The default setting for Tolerance is 32 (to reset tools to their default settings, hold the mouse down over the tool icon to the left of the status bar until a menu drops down and choose Reset All Tools).

With the tolerance set at 32, Photoshop will select all the pixels that are 32 shades lighter, and 32 shades darker than the selected pixel. If Photoshop is selecting too many pixels (or if you are working with a low contrast image), reduce the Tolerance. If Photoshop is not selecting enough pixels (or if you are working with a high contrast image), increase the Tolerance.

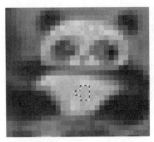
Tolerance : 2

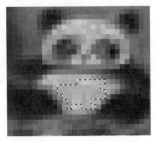
Tolerance : 10

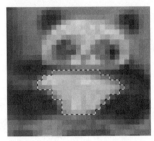
Tolerance : 32

Tolerance : 100

As with the other Selection tools, settings that are available in the Magic Wand Tool Options Bar are Add To, Subtract From, and Intersect Existing Selections.

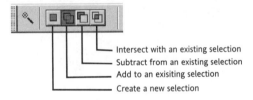

Intersect with an existing selection
Subtract from an existing selection
Add to an exisiting selection
Create a new selection

Additional options are **Anti-aliasing, Contiguous** and **Use All Layers**.

Check for an Anti-aliased selection

If the Contiguous box is unchecked, Photoshop selects all pixels of a similar color anywhere in the image. If the box is checked, it only selects adjacent similarly colored pixels.

If you are working on an image that has layers, the Use All Layers option allows you to select similar colors throughout all the layers (if the box is checked, it treats the file as though it were flattened).

Tolerance: 50 Contiguous: checked   Tolerance: 50 Contiguous: unchecked

To make a selection using the Magic Wand, select the magic wand tool from the Toolbox, modify the settings in the status bar if need be, and then click on the pixel that you want Photoshop to make the selection from.

Moving Selections

Once a selection has been made, there are many ways to move it to another location in the document or into another open document. In Photoshop the marquee can be separated from the image, and so can be moved independently from the pixels it selects. It is important to be aware what we are moving when using the following set of actions! In Photoshop it is possible to:

- Move the marquee (the flashing black and white lines) to another place in the document or into another open document.

- Move the selected pixels, leaving the original area either transparent or showing the background color.

- Move the selected pixels, copying them to another location in the document or into another document.

Moving a Marquee

You can move a marquee by doing the following:

- Using one of the Selection tools, select a part of your image.

- Once the selection is closed and it has turned into black and white lines, move the cursor over the selection. The cursor will change to an arrow with a box next to it.

> TIP: To move the marquee more accurately you can use the arrow keys on your keypad to move it pixel by pixel. This also means that the marquee moves in a straight line.

● This means you can now move (by clicking and dragging) the marquee to another part of the document. The marquee can be used as a pastry-cutter to select a new area of pixels, which will be the same shape as the original selection. The original area of pixels will be deselected. The marquee can also be dragged into another open document.

Moving Selected Pixels

1. Use one of the selection tools to select part of your image.

   Move the cursor inside the selection and hold down the Ctrl/⌘ key (the cursor will change to a black arrow with scissors next to it)

2. Holding down the Ctrl/z key, click and drag the selection to another area of your image or into a new document (alternatively, once you have made the selection change to the Move tool and the same cursor will appear, enabling you to move the selected pixels).

3. As you move the selected pixels, notice that the area where the marquee was originally now shows the background color (or, if you are working with a file that has layers, a lower layer) and is no longer selected. The selected pixels remain selected and free to move until they are deselected.

Copying a Selection to a New Location

1. Using one of the selection tools, select part of your image.

2. Move the selection tool over the selected pixels and hold down the Ctrl/z-Alt keys. The cursor will change to a black arrowhead sitting over a white arrowhead (alternatively, select the move tool and hold down the Alt key.).

3. Holding down the appropriate key, click and drag the selection to another part of the file, or into a new document. The selected pixels will be copied and moved to another area of the document leaving the originally selected pixels in place. As long as the pixels remain selected, it is possible to move, copy and move the selection as many times you like.

Copying Selections

It is possible to copy selected pixels in a number of ways;

- By using keyboard shortcuts in conjunction with Selection tools or the Move tool

- By using Ctrl/⌘.

- By using the Edit menu.

Copying Selected Pixels to a New Layer

- Using one of the Selection tools, select part of your image.

- Move the selection tool over the selected area and hold down Ctrl/z and Alt keys. The cursor will change to a black arrowhead sitting over a white arrowhead. Alternatively, select the Move tool and hold down the Alt key.

> ● ● *TIP: Photoshop automatically*
> ● *pastes the pixels into a new*
> ○ *layer. This can cause confusion, as it is the layer that has been pasted that remains active. If you are using this method, keep the Layer palette open and flatten when necessary, or, make sure that you are working on the right layer.*

Holding down the appropriate key, click and drag the selection to another part of the file, or into a new document. The selected pixels will be copied and moved to another area of the document leaving the originally selected pixels in place. As long as the pixels remain selected (the black and white lines are still flashing) it is possible to move, copy and move the selection as many times you like.

Copying

- Using one of the Selection tools, select part of your image.

- Once your selection has been made, hit Ctrl/⌘-C or Edit > Copy. The selected pixels are now stored into memory and can be pasted back into your file or into another file. The pixels remain stored until you make another selection or purge the memory. This can be useful if you want to paste the pixels into another application.

- The command for pasting pixels is Ctrl/⌘-V or to **Edit > Paste**.

Transformations

To **Transform** the marquee (and NOT the selected pixels), go to one of the **Select > Transform** menu options.

Or, Right/Ctrl click a selection when a selection tool is in use and select **Transform Selection** from In the Select menu there is another sub-menu called Modify that allows further, subtle modifications to marquees.

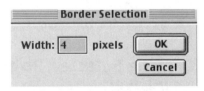

- **Border** allows you to select the border of the selection. When you choose this option a window is launched asking you how many pixels wide the border should be. The value will depend on the resolution of your image: if the resolution of your image is high, enter a high value; if the resolution of your image is low, enter a lower value

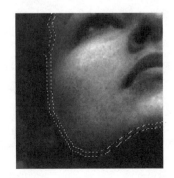

● **Smooth** softens the edges of a selection and prevents jagged lines.

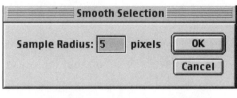

● **Expand** allows you to increase the size of the selection by a precise number of pixels.

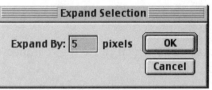

● **Contract** allows you to make the selection smaller by a precise number of pixels.

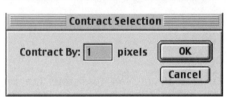

Transforming Selected Pixels

To Transform not only the marquee, but also the pixels inside it, go to **Edit > Transform**. Here you will find the same Transform options that are available in the Transform Selection menu. This menu becomes active whenever a selection is made.

Transformations are made in the same way as when transforming marquees, either by dragging the corner on the bounding box, or by entering values into the Status bar.

> *TIP: Beware of making large scale changes to selections as they may stand out and look ugly. This is because, as you stretch the selection, Photoshop will 'make up' the pixels.*

Transforming Selections

Once a selection has been made, it is possible to **transform** (Scale, Rotate, Distort, Skew, Distort, Perspective, Rotate 180, Rotate 90, Rotate 90 CC, Flip Horizontal, Flip Vertical) both the marquee and the selected pixels. Remember that a marquee is only the flashing black and white line – the shape of the selection – and it can be treated independently of the selected pixels. Marquees are transformed via the Select menu

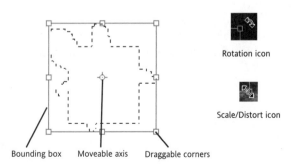

Rotation icon

Scale/Distort icon

Bounding box   Moveable axis   Draggable corners

and selected pixels are transformed via the Edit menu.

Say we have a selection that looks like this:

Scale: allows you resize the marquee or selected pixels.

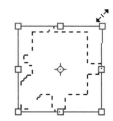

Rotate: allows you to rotate the marquee or selected pixels around a moveable axis point.

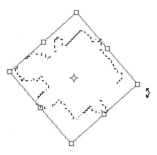

Distort: allows you to pull the corners in and out and so alter the shape of the marquee or selected pixels.

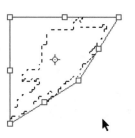

Skew: allows you to change the shape of the marquee or selected pixels by moving its sides.

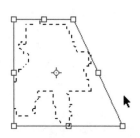

Perspective: allows you to change the shape of the marquee or selected pixels by pulling in adjacent corners by the same amount, giving the illusion of changing perspective.

Rotate 180: rotates the marquee or selected pixels around a moveable axis point 180 degrees.

Rotate 90 Right: rotates the marquee or selected pixels around a moveable axis point 90 degrees clockwise.

Rotate 90 Left: rotates the marquee or selected pixels around a moveable axis point 90 degrees counter clockwise.

Flip Horizontal mirrors the marquee horizontally or selected pixels around a moveable axis.

Flip Vertical mirrors the marquee vertically or selected pixels around a moveable axis:

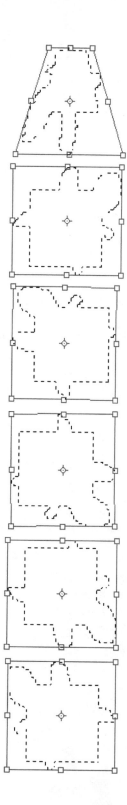

Selecting the Inverse

If you have a number of small details in your image that you want to protect from a change that you want to make to a larger part of the image, it may be tedious to spend a long time drawing large selections. An easier way is to make a selection around the small area, and then **invert** the selection. This means that everything is selected, apart from the small area or areas that you want to protect.

If you have made a selection you want to invert, either:

- Click **Select > Inverse**.

- Right/Control click and choose **Select Inverse** from the menu.

- Ctrl/⌘-Shift-I.

Fill

If you want to fill a selection with a flat color or with a pattern you can do so by Right/Ctrl-clicking a selection and then choose **Edit > Fill** from the menu. This launches another menu that allows you to select a color, blending mode, and opacity level.

This works in exactly the same way as if you had selected the Fill tool from the Toolbox (see Chapter 1), but it just saves changing tools.

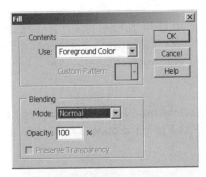

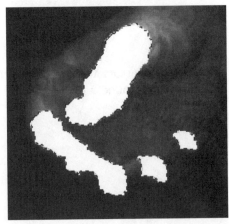

Stroke

If you want your marquee to turn into a line of color, it is possible to do so using the **Stroke** command. Choose **Edit > Stroke** from the menu. A window will be launched giving a number of options – the color and width of the fill line, whether the line should be outside, inside or centered to the marquee.

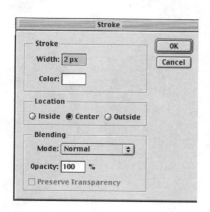

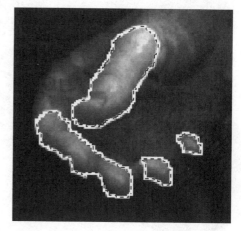

Conclusion

We have now more or less covered all the different ways to select pixels in Photoshop using the selection tools. By familiarizing yourself with these different tools and understanding how they work, you should build up a strong vocabulary of ways to select pixels in Photoshop, depending on the nature of your image.

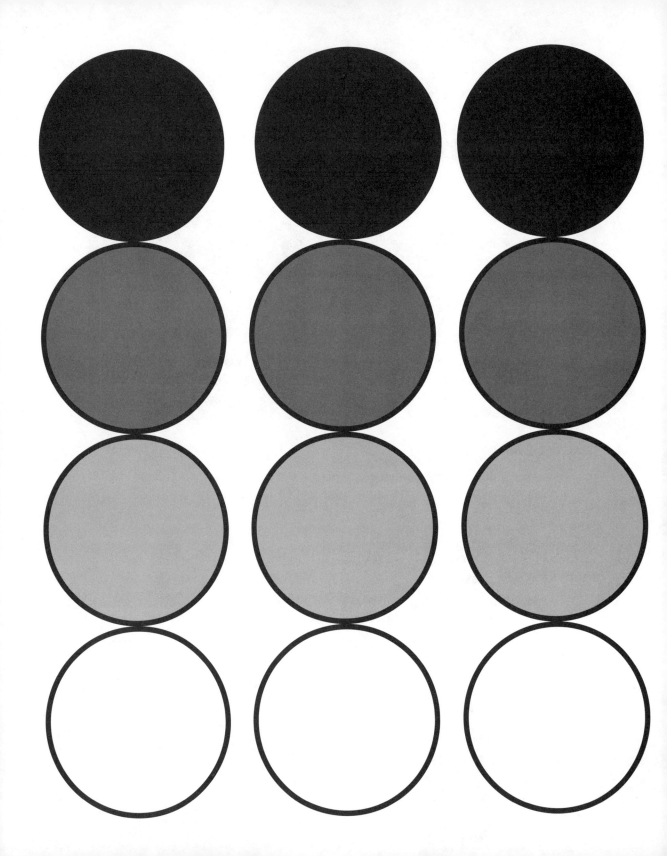

CHAPTER 3
MONTAGE

Introduction

Layers are very powerful tools, as they allow a lot of freedom in the creative process. There is no limit to the number of layers you can create, plus there are endless ways to manipulate those layers, and to use them to interact with other layers.

Although it is possible to create many complicated effects with Photoshop layers, their beauty lies in their simplicity and ease of use. The logic of layers has long been in use by traditional animators and image creators. I am confident that once you have been introduced to Layers, you will never go back!

The Layers Palette

The Layers palette is a free-floating window where all the information about layers in a document is stored. To open the Layers palette, (if it is not already open in the bottom right hand corner of your screen) go to the Palette Well and drag the Layers palette out.

If there is no document open, the Layers palette will not list any layers and all the palette options will be dimmed.

When a new, blank document is opened, there will be just one layer that will automatically be called *Background* and some of the options will become active.

When a document that contains many layers is opened, all the layers are listed, and depending which layer is highlighted, all of the options become active.

As I explained in the introduction, layers can be thought of as sheets of acetate with different elements on them. The Layers palette displays the different layers (or sheets of acetate) in stacked order. The layer at the top of the stack/list is the top sheet of acetate and the bottom layer (usually called the Background layer) is the bottom sheet of acetate. In the example here, big yellow flower would be the top sheet of acetate, and Background would be the bottom sheet.

Each Layer is represented by a small picture icon showing the image pixels the layer contains and, next to it, the layer's name. Transparency in Photoshop is indicated by small gray and white squares (unless you have specified otherwise in the Preferences). This means that all the areas in the layers that do not contain image information are transparent and displayed in the picture icon as gray and white squares.

There are a number of different icons and buttons in the Layers Palette.

To the left hand side of the listed layers there are two boxes. The left of the two boxes tells you whether the layer is visible, or, turned on. If the layer is visible, a small icon of an eye appears in the box. To turn visibility of a layer on or off to make it easier to work with other layers, click the box.

The right of the two boxes tells you whether you can paint on the layer (this is indicated by an icon of a brush). This symbol will appear if the layer is active (to make a layer active click on its icon or name and it will become highlighted). This also shows whether a layer is linked to another layer (with an icon of a chain). To link a layer, click on the box. Linking two layers together allows you to move or transform two layers

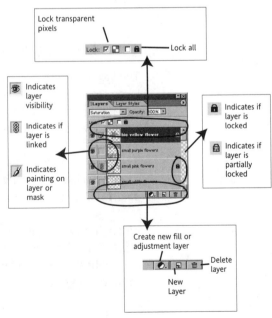

at the same time, it does not, however, allow you to paint or apply filters to two layers simultaneously.

At the top of the Palette there is a row of boxes that allow you to lock the transparency, the image pixels, the position or the entire layer. To lock, or partially lock a layer, check the appropriate box.

If a layer is locked it will display an icon to the right of its name. If the layer is only partially locked (if only its transparency pixels are locked), then it will display an unfilled lock icon. If the layer is completely locked (the Lock All box at the top of the palette has been checked), then a filled lock will be displayed.

At the bottom of the palette is a row of icons that allow you to delete a layer, to create a new layer, create a new adjustment layer. These icons are for more advanced use of layers and will be addressed at later stages in this chapter.

Customizing the Layers Palette

It is possible to change the look of the palette to suit our preferred way of working. If you have a small monitor, for example, you can optimize screen space by asking for small picture icons in your layers palette, or even no icon at all. If you want to see what is in your layers easily without having to strain your eyes, you can select a larger icon.

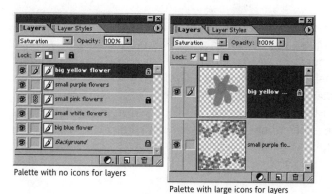

Palette with no icons for layers

Palette with large icons for layers

1. To change the size of the icon click on the little arrow in the top right-hand corner of the palette and choose Palette Options from the menu.

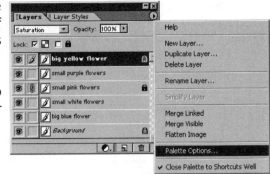

2. A window will appear giving the option to choose from 3 different sizes of icons, or none.

3. Once you have checked the appropriate radio button and clicked OK, the palette will be restored with your chosen size of icon (if any).

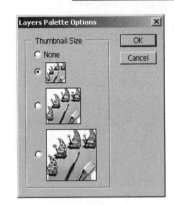

Creating a New Layer

There are a number of ways to create a new layer in Photoshop:

● Click on the New Layer icon in the bottom right hand corner of the Layers palette.

● Go to Layer > New > Layer.

● Press Ctrl/⌘-Shift-N.

● Click the little arrow in the top right hand corner of the Layer palette and selecting New Layer.

TIP: When a document has layers, the title bar displays the name of the active layer.

When you create a new layer in one of the first three ways, a window will be launched that allows you to give a name to your layer and to color code it (there are also the options to select a layer **Mode** and **Opacity**. These options will be explained later in the chapter). It is good practice to name your layers as it can easily get very confusing and difficult to remember what each layer is if the elements are too small to be seen in the palette icon.

Choosing to create a layer by pressing the New Layer icon in the Layers palette does not launch this window, and a layer will appear in the layers palette as a numbered layer. If you want to name or rename a layer, go to the **Layer** menu and select **Rename Layer...** and a window will launch allowing you to name the layer.

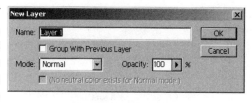

Once you have created a new layer in any of the above ways it will appear in your layer palette, but, as layers are transparent, you will not be able to see it in your image window. The new layer automatically becomes the active layer (the layer you are working on).

When a new layer is created it is placed directly above the active layer in the layers palette (so it will not necessarily be the top layer).

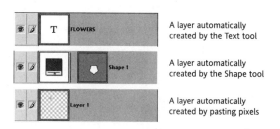

A layer automatically created by the Text tool

A layer automatically created by the Shape tool

A layer automatically created by pasting pixels

> TIP: When you use the text tool, create a vector shape, or copy and paste pixels into a document, a new layer is automatically created and will sit directly above the layer you were working on when the action was performed.

Layering a Number of Objects

Once a new layer has been created, it can be drawn in using one of the painting tools, or by filling a marquee. Once image pixels are in the layer they can then be moved, transformed, adjusted (color), and have effects applied to them. Until image pixels are present on the layer, Photoshop reads it as empty, making any **Adjust**, **Transform** or **Filter** commands unavailable. If you do try to adjust an empty layer an alert window will launch reminding you that there are no pixels to adjust.

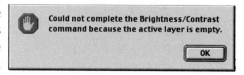

To start placing image pixels on a layer, make sure that the Layers palette is open and that the layer that you want to work on is active (it should be highlighted and there should be a paintbrush icon next to it).

Either:

● Select a Painting tool and draw in the image window:

● Or select a Marquee tool, draw a marquee and then fill it:

Notice that the drawing or the shape you have created in the image window can now be seen in the Layer Palette icon.

You can create and work on as many layers as you want. To continue building up layers simply ask for a new layer by clicking the New Layer button.

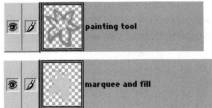

Duplicating Layers

It can be very useful (and time saving) to duplicate layers. If, for example, as in the illustration, your layers contain similar objects, it may be easier to modify an existing layer, rather than redraw it. Layers can be duplicated in a number of ways:

● Drag the layer you want to duplicate onto the New Layer icon at the bottom of the Layer Palette.

● Make the layer you want to duplicate active in the Layers palette, then go to the Layer menu and choose Duplicate Layer

● Make the layer you want to duplicate active in the Layers palette, then select Duplicate Layer from the palette menu

Each of these options will result in a new layer being created in your Layer palette that contains the same image pixels as the layer you duplicated. The layer will automatically be placed above the duplicated layer, and 'copy' will be placed at the end of the layer name.

Moving Layers Up & Down the List

If you were working on a number of different sheets of clear acetate to build an image, you would no doubt be constantly changing the order of the sheets to see how the different elements worked together. Similarly, when building a Photoshop image with layers you want to be able to try different layers on top of others or move one under another.

It is very easy to re-arrange your layers; **simply click and drag** the layers to a different position in the list. This allows you to try out many variations of your image without having to re-create it, or save different versions of it. If, for example, as in the illustration, you had made an image of flowers and kept all the different flowers on different layers, you could quickly see which flowers sit better over others, just by clicking and dragging layers up and down the list.

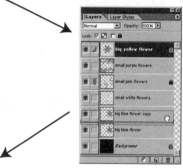

Click on the name of the layer you want to move (it will change color) and then drag it up/down the list, keeping the mouse down until a black bar appears where you want the layer to be (in this case, above the blue flower).

When you let go of the mouse the layer will be in a different position (above the blue flower).

The Background layer, which is the layer that a document opens with, cannot be moved until it has been unlocked. To unlock a Background layer, double click it and rename it in the **New Layer** window that appears.

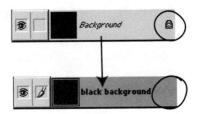

Moving and Scaling Layers

When a layer is active, its image pixels can be moved and transformed without having to manually select them.

Moving a layer

To move the contents of a layer, make sure that the layer you want to move is active by highlighting it in the Layers palette and then select the Move tool in the Toolbox.

Click and drag the layer until it is in the right place. When the Move tool is in use you can also use the arrows on your keypad to gently nudge the layer into place pixel by pixel.

TIP: Press the shift key as you nudge to move a layer by 10 pixels at a time.

If you move the image pixels that are on the layer off the canvas, they are still saved and can be moved back at a later time (even if you close and then reopen the document). The layer icon in the Layers palette however only displays the image pixels that are on the canvas.

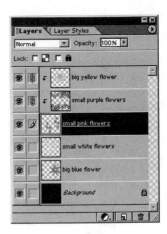

To change the order of more than one layer, group the layers you want to move (by linking the layers you want to move and choosing **Group Linked** from the layer menu). You will then be able to move the group of layers to a new position in the list. To ungroup the layers, select the layer at the bottom of the group and select Ungroup from the layer menu.

Transforming a layer

The same transform options that are available for selected pixels (see Chapter 2) are also available for an active layer. So long as a layer is not locked, its image pixels can be transformed (Scale, Rotate, Distort, Skew, Perspective, Rotate 180, Rotate 90, Rotate 90 CC, Flip Horizontal, Flip Vertical).

To transform the pixels in a layer, make the layer active (click on it in the Layers palette) then go to Image > Transform > Free Transform.

Transform takes you to a menu from which you can select Scale, Rotate, Distort, Skew, Perspective, Rotate 180, Rotate 90, Rotate 90 CC, Flip Horizontal or Flip Vertical.

Pull and drag the corners (or nodes) to perform the transformation. The cursor will change according to which transformation is taking place.

Rotation icon   Stretch/Resize icon

A bounding box will appear around the image pixels allowing you to perform transformations manually by dragging the corners of the bounding box and by moving the axis. The icon changes, depending on the kind of transformation taking place.

The Tool Options Bar will also change, allowing you to input values into the Transform boxes.

When you have completed transforming the layer, either press return, or click the tick to the right of the Tool Options Bar. The bounding box will disappear and the transformed pixels will remain in the layer.

Managing Layers

Once you start building up a number of layers things can get very confusing, not to mention very slow, as the file size increases with every new layer you make. You may feel that you want to delete some of your layers, or combine them

Deleting Layers

To delete a layer from your palette:

- Make the layer you want to delete active and select Delete Layer from the Layer menu

- Make the layer you want to delete active and select Delete Layer from the Layer palette menu

- Drag the layer you want to delete onto the Wastebasket icon in the bottom right hand corner of the layer palette.

TIP: To delete a lot of layers at once, link them, then merge them before deleting.

Merging layers

Merging layers allows you to put the image pixels from two or more layers onto the same layer. There are a two ways to merge layers together – by Merging Linked or Merging Visible. These options are stored in the Layer Menu and the Layer Palette menu.

Merging linked layers

To merge layers by linking them, select one of the layers that you want to merge. Then click in the right of the two boxes to the left of the layer's icon. The link icon should appear in this box.

When you have linked all the layers you want to merge with the active layer, then either:

- Go to the Palette menu and select Merge Linked.

- Select Merge Linked from the Layer menu.

- Press Ctrl/⌘-E on your keypad.

All the image pixels from the linked layers will now be in the active layer and can be moved, transformed, or adjusted together.

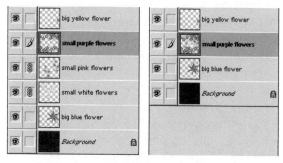

Merge linked

Merging visible Layers

Personally, I find this the best way to merge layers as it means you know exactly what your layers will look like when they are merged. Turn the visibility off for all the layers you don't want to merge (so that you can only see the layers to be merged in the image window). To turn the visibility of a layer off, click in the left of the two boxes to the left of the layer's icon. Then either:

- Go to the Palette menu and select Merge Visible from the list.

- Select Merge Visible from the Layer menu.

- Or press Ctrl/⌘-Shift-E on your keypad.

TIP: Notice how the file size decreases when you merge layers together.

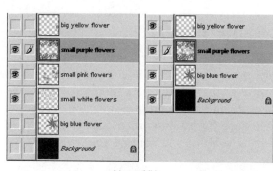

Merge visible

Flattening Layers

Flattening Layers merges all of the layers into a Background. If there were any areas in the image that were transparent (there were still gray and white squares visible even when all the layers were turned on), they will flatten to be white. To flatten an image, either go to the palette menu and select Flatten Image, or select Flatten Image from the Layer menu.

If any of the layers have had their visibility turned off when you ask for the document to be flattened, Photoshop will ask you whether you want them to be discarded (not included in the flattened image).

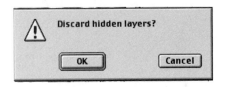

TIP: Only flatten your image when you are sure you have finished working on the image, OR, even better, save a version of your image with layers before you flatten.

Saving Layers

ALWAYS save a file that contains layers as a .PSD file, otherwise all your layer information will be lost. All other file formats flatten layers as they save. If you do try and save a document that has layers in a format other than .PSD, Photoshop will remind you that you will lose your layers.

Adjusting the Opacity of a Layer

Opacity is the opposite of Transparency. If something is 100% opaque (or 0% transparent), we cannot see anything beneath it. If something if 70% opaque (or 30% transparent), we can make out what is beneath it, a bit like a layer of tissue paper. If something is 30% opaque (or 70 % transparent), we can see through it completely as if through a soft shadow. Changing the opacity level of a layer is very useful and can lead to very nice effects.

Yellow Flower - 100% Opacity

Yellow Flower - 70% Opacity

Yellow Flower - 30% Opacity

To change the opacity of a layer, make it active via the Layers palette and enter an Opacity percentage next to the Opacity box at the top of the Layers palette. Alternatively, click on the little arrow next to the Opacity box and use the slider.

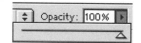

Blending Mode

The blending mode decides how layers interact with each other – how the image pixels of a layer blends with the image pixels in the lower layers. Modes can make a layer darken or lighten areas of the layers beneath them or tint to radically change the colors of layers beneath them and even invert them. It is often hard to predict how changing the mode of a layer will affect the lower layers; the best way to learn about them is to play!

The list of blending modes is to the left of opacity. By default layers will be set to normal. To change the mode, click on where it says normal and a list of the modes drops down. Select a mode from the list and the active layer will automatically change to this mode.

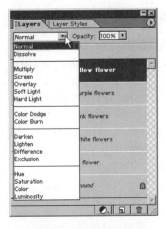

Normal: This is the default setting. There is no blending with this option.

Dissolve: This creates a grainy, dry brush effect in the layer. To increase the graininess of the layer, reduce the opacity.

Multiply: This 'multiplies' the layer with the layer beneath it. If the image pixels of the layer are dark, the image pixels on the layers below become darker as it removes any lighter parts of the lower layers. If the image pixels of the layer are light, it becomes very transparent

Screen: This makes the layer lighten lower layers.

Overlay: Overlay is a combination of the Multiply mode and the Screen mode; it darkens the dark areas and lightens the light areas of lower layers.

Soft Light: Soft light is similar to Overlay; it lightens a lower layer if the pixels are light and darkens them if they are dark.

Hard Light works like Overlay but the pixels are much more opaque.

Color Dodge: Color Dodge brightens the lower layers if the pixels are light but has little effect when they are dark. Mid tone pixels fill in the dark areas and tint the light areas of lower layers.

Color Burn: This is the opposite of Color Dodge; it darkens the lower layer if the pixels are dark, but has little effect if they are light. Color Burn looks like ink spilled on to an image; dark inks obliterate the image, light inks stain.

Darken: Darken looks at the pixels of the layer and those beneath it and decides which are the darkest. The darkest color remains.

Lighten: This is the opposite of the Darken mode. If the pixels in the layer are lighter than those in the lower layers, then it stays, if it is darker, then they remain.

Difference: Difference looks at the pixels in the layer and those of the lower layers and subtracts the brighter colored pixels from the darker colored pixels. This results in the colors being inverted. The brighter the pixels of the layer in Difference mode, the more dramatic the negative effect in the lower layer.

Exclusion: This is very similar to Difference but there is less contrast in the areas of inverted pixels.

Hue: The layer tints lower layers with its color shade.

Saturation: The saturation level of the layer is applied to the lower layers. The brighter the layer, the more saturated the lower layers become.

Color: The color and saturation of the layer are applied to the lower layers.

Luminosity: Luminosity applies the grayscale value of the layer to the lower layers.

The Layer Styles Palette

In addition to being able to control the opacity and the mode of a layer, you can also apply a style to it. Photoshop offers a selection of different styles that can transform your image (such as bevels, metallic, shiny, bumpy, gradients, glows and drop shadows). At worst, application of these preset styles can be obvious and tacky but, at best, by modifying their settings, styles can bring even the most boring and flat image magically to life.

The power of Photoshop **Styles** has now been incorporated into the Layers Styles palette. This not only allows you to apply Photoshop's pre-set styles to a layer but, in conjunction with the Layers palette, also to modify the existing styles and create new ones.

To launch the Layer Style Palette drag it from the Palette Well. It might be easy to tuck it behind the layers palette by dragging it to the darker grey area next to the Layer's palette tab.

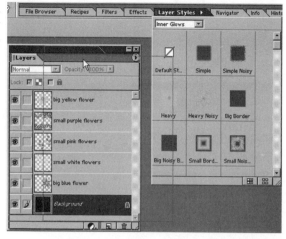

Complex Preset Styles

The layer's palette features a number of preset styles, which might be just the thing you're looking for. To apply one of the styles:

1. Using the Layers palette select the layer you wish to apply the style to.

2. Switch to the Layer Styles palette.

3. Using the drop-down menu, select the **Complex** styles – these are the preset ones.

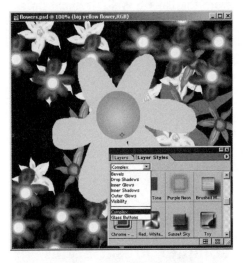

4. Select the style of your choice (we've gone for brushed metal).

5. Now return to the layers palette. You will notice that an "f" symbol has appeared to the right of the layer's name to indicate it has a style applied to it.

TIP: If you do a search on the Internet for Photoshop styles you will find many websites that allow you to download more styles.

Other Styles

The layers palette also features a series of standard effects that the user can modify to create their own effect. These are accessed from the dropdown menu at the top of the palette.

Bevels: These are inner or outer edges that apply a 3D-like edge to shapes.

Drop shadows: Effects that appear behind the shapes on a layer.

Inner Glows: Effects that appear around the inside edges of shapes on a layer.

Inner Shadows: Appear like glows inside, but darker, to give something the appearance of negative depth.

Outer Glows: Give an object a halo-effect.

Visibility: An alternative to using the opacity to make a layer see-through.

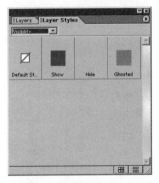

Glass Buttons: A combination of color-fills, inner glows and inner shadows to give a glass ball like effect.

Affecting the Styles

1. To use one of these effects, select the layer you wish to apply it to and then select the Layer Styles palette as before.

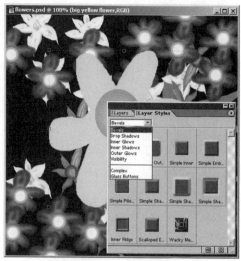

2. Apply an effect of your choice (we've gone for simple inner bevel).

3. Return to the Layers palette and double click on the 'f' that has appeared to the right of the layer's name.

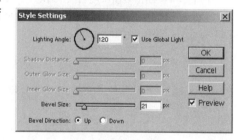

4. Reduce the size of the bevel you have created by dragging the Bevel Size slider at the bottom of the box.

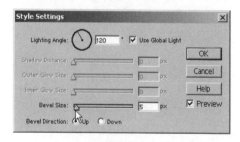

5. You can also alter the apparent lighting angle by dragging the 'clock' at the top of the window (or reverse it completely by pressing the Bevel Direction switch at the bottom).

6. When you are happy with the changes you have made, click OK.

Combining Styles

It is possible to apply more than one of these styles to a single layer – one from each of the top 6 categories on the drop down menu. More options will then become available in the Style Settings box.

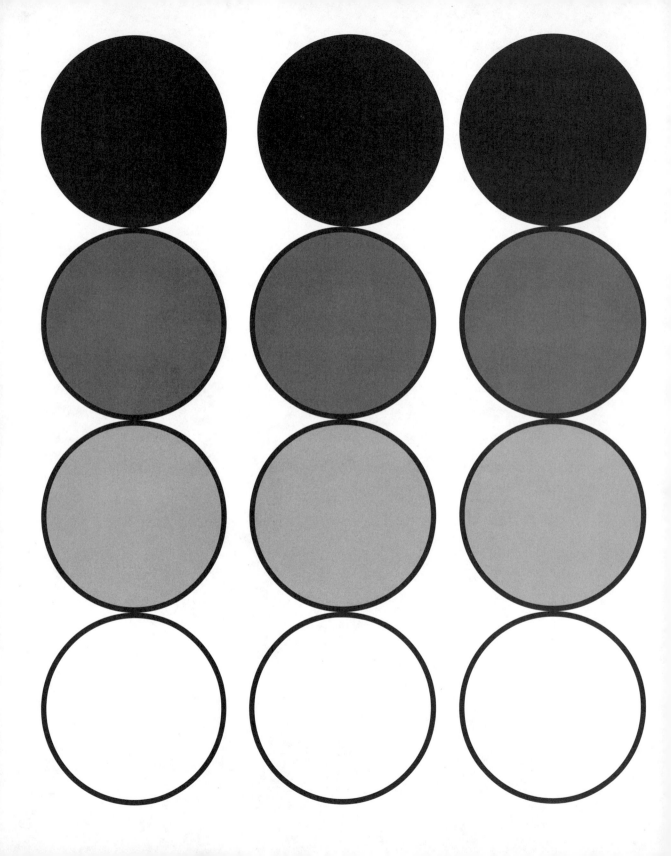

CHAPTER 4
TEXT AND EFFECTS

Photoshop Elements allows you to enter text directly in the image window. Plus, as with everything in Photoshop, there is no end of effects that can be applied to text. Text can have Styles applied to it, be warped, transformed, and, if this still not enough, rasterized and then manipulated even further.

In short, text is not only logical but also fun in Photoshop. So, with no further ado, let's arm ourselves with enough knowledge to write what has to be written and then play!

Typing in a Basic Word

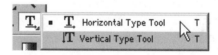

To apply text to an image, select the Text tool from the Toolbox. Text can either be written traditionally (the default) or downwards (letters above each other). Even after you've selected you can switch back using the Text Orientation button on the Tool Options bar.

vertical

On the left hand side of the Tool Options Bar are two other buttons,

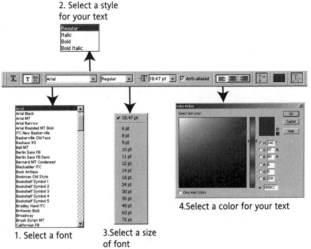

Write text

Write selection

To create normal text, select Create a Text layer and Horizontal text (we will learn more of the options later in this chapter). Now click anywhere on your image and a cursor will flash where you clicked. This means that you can now type.

Before doing so however, you can decide the font, size, and color of your text. This can be done via the Text Options bar which becomes active when the Text tool is selected. Notice that once you have clicked inside the Image window, the Options bar has changed and the options for creating a text layer, creating a selection, horizontal text, and vertical text have disappeared.

2. Select a style for your text

1. Select a font

3. Select a size of font

4. Select a color for your text

- Select a font from the drop down menu on the far left side of the Options bar (you will only be able to select fonts that are stored on your system).

- Select a style for your font (*italic,* **bold,** etc) from the drop down menu to the right of the Font menu. Not all fonts will allow you to select different styles.

- Select a size for your font from the drop down menu to the right of the Style menu. To change the units for your type go to **Edit > Preferences > Units and Rulers** and select a unit from the **Type** drop down menu.

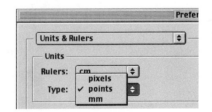

Select a color for your text by clicking the color box to the right hand side of the Options bar, which launches the color picker. To select a color use the sliders or enter a value (to learn more about selecting colors see Chapter 1).

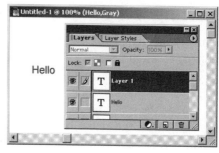

You will notice that there is an option available for anti-aliasing. Leave it on for now. Anti-aliasing will be discussed later in this chapter. Once you have selected the font, style and size of your text, return to the image menu and start typing. In Photoshop, text is written directly onto the canvas (in previous versions it was entered and edited in a separate window).

Open the Layers palette. Notice how a new layer has been created with a T icon. Photoshop automatically places text on a new layer.

You may want to move your layer to a different area of the image window whilst you are typing. To do this, move the cursor away from the text and the cursor will change to the move icon. It is now possible to click and drag the text to another area of the image.

TIP: As text is created as a text layer it can be moved at any time by selecting the Move tool and clicking and dragging the layer.

Once you have finished entering the text, click the checkmark to the right of the Options bar, or click on another layer to commit the text to the layer.

TIP: Until the text is committed to the layer (or it is rejected), it will be not possible to continue working in Photoshop. You can reject the text by clicking the 'X' to the right of the Options bar.

Notice in the Layers palette that the name of the text layer is the content of the text.

Now that the layer has been committed, a new text layer will be created whenever you click in the image window (for as long as the Text tool is in use).

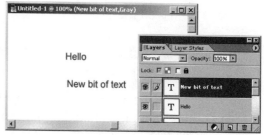

Editing a Text Layer

Once a text layer has been created, its contents can easily be edited, at any time, and as many times as is needed, without loss of quality in the text.

To change the font, style or color of the text, select the layer in the Layers palette and make the changes you want via the Text tool Options bar (if the Text Options bar is not active, click on the Text Tool in the Toolbox).

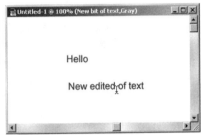

To edit the content of the text, or, change the font, color and size of only part of the text, make the layer active, select the Text tool and click inside or highlight the text you want to change.

When you have finished editing the text, click on the checkmark to the right of the Options bar and press return on your keypad to commit the changes to the text layer.

Loading Text from Other Sources

To use text that has been written in another program in a Photoshop image (i.e. a word processing document) without retyping it all in Photoshop, you can copy and paste it in.

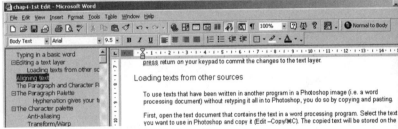

1. First, open the text document that contains the text in a word processing program.

2. Select the text you want to use in Photoshop and copy it (CTRL/⌘-C). The copied text will be stored on the clipboard.

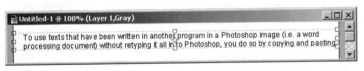

3. Now open the Photoshop document (in Photoshop), select the text tool, click on the Image and then **Edit > Paste**, or

> TIP: This is a good method to ensure correct spelling, as Photoshop has no spell check. If you are paranoid about incorrect spelling, prepare your text in another program that has a spell checker and then copy and paste it in.

CTRL/⌘-V. The text will appear in the image window and in the layer palette as a text layer.

Formatting Text

Photoshop has formatting tools that allow you to justify your text. To make your lines of text line up to the right, left or center, use Photoshop's alignment tools, which are in the Text Tool Options Bar.

To align your text, simply click on one of these buttons when the text layer is active.

Align center
Align right → ← Align left

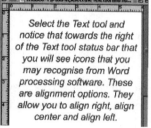

Select the Text tool and notice that towards the right of the Text tool status bar that you will see icons that you may recognise from Word processing software. These are alignment options. They allow you to align right, align center and align left.

Select the Text tool and notice that towards the right of the Text tool status bar that you will see icons that you may recognise from Word processing software. These are alignment options. They allow you to align right, align center and align left.

Anti-aliasing

Photoshop is a bitmap program, so its images are made up of square pixels. This can often be a problem when using text in Photoshop because text is made up of many rounded lines which, by definition, bitmap graphics cannot create. When working at a low resolution or zooming into an image we can see that the rounded parts of letters are converted into ugly jagged lines. To reduce these ugly edges, Photoshop gives us an anti-aliasing option.

> TIP: This effect is especially useful for screen-based work, but can create fuzzy edges when printing.

Anti-aliasing softens the hard jagged edges by looking at the edge and working out how much of each of the edge pixels would be covered by the diagonal line and draws that pixel as an intermediate shade between background and foreground. If, for example, your text is black and your background is white, Photoshop substitutes the outside pixels for shades of gray to make the transition smoother.

> TIP: As text layers are vector based (not bitmap images) they can be transformed and warped with no lack of quality in the text. The anti-aliasing will be automatically updated after each change

No anti-aliasing

anti-aliased

☑ Anti-aliased

Transforming Text

As text sits on its own layer, it can be transformed as though it were a layer (rotated, rescaled, distorted, flipped etc.). In addition to transforming your text, you can also warp it. Photoshop has very powerful Text Warping tools which can all be modified to your specifications. This allows a great amount of freedom and hours of fun playing around with your text!

To transform your text, select the layer of text that you want to transform and go to **Edit > Free Transform** (Ctrl/⌘-T). A bounding box will appear around text and by pulling out the corners you can stretch, squash and resize your text.

When you move the cursor to the corners, the cursor will change to a rounded icon that allows you to rotate the text.

If you hold down the Ctrl/⌘ key, the cursor changes to a single arrow, allowing you to skew the text.

When you have finished performing the transformation, click on the checkmark on the Tool Options Bar or press return to commit the transformation

For further transformations, again select the Text layer that you want to transform and go to the Image menu for other transformations.

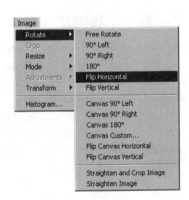

To perform one of these transformations select it from the list. Remember to commit the transformation when you are satisfied (by clicking on the tick to the right of the Options bar or by pressing return on your keypad).

Warping Text

Warping text allows you to shape your text in many ways. To the right hand side of the text Tool Options bar is the **Warp Text** button.

To warp your text, select the text layer that you want to adjust, click the warp button and the Warp window will launch.

Warp Text

Style: ✓ None

○ Hori

Bend:

Horizon

Vertical

Arc
Arc Lower
Arc Upper
Arch
Bulge
Shell Lower
Shell Upper
Flag
Wave
Fish
Rise
Fisheye
Inflate
Squeeze
Twist

OK

Cancel

From here you can select one of the warping options and then modify the settings until you achieve the warp effect that you want. The warp previews in the image window, so move the dialog box so that you can see the Image window. The settings for Warping are:

● **Horizontal /Vertical**: Determines whether the warp is applied to the text horizontally or vertically. To select one of the options, click the radio button.

● **Bend**: Determines how strong the warp effect is. A positive number makes it warp the direction depicted in the style menue. A negative value makes it warp in the opposite direction.

● **Horizontal Distortion**: Distorts the text horizontally: A positive value makes it larger on the right, a negative value, larger to the left.

● **Vertical Distortion**: Distorts the text vertically, a positive value makes the text distort downwards, a negative value, upwards.

To change the settings either enter values or use the sliders. The settings for each of the Warping options are the same for each shape, although it is not always possible to select between a horizontal or vertical warp.

Styles

Arc: Text forms into the shape of an arc. The arc is formed from the centerline of the text.

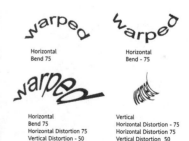

Horizontal
Bend 75

Horizontal
Bend - 75

Horizontal
Bend 75
Horizontal Distortion 75
Vertical Distortion - 50

Vertical
Horizontal Distortion - 75
Horizontal Distortion 75
Vertical Distortion 50

Arc Lower: Text forms into the shape of an arc. The arcs are formed from the baseline of the text.

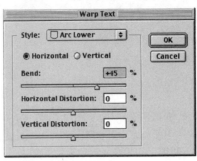

Horizontal
Bend 75

Horizontal
Bend - 75

Horizontal
Bend 75
Horizontal Distortion 75
Vertical Distortion - 50

Vertical
Horizontal Distortion - 75
Horizontal Distortion 75
Vertical Distortion 50

Arc Upper: Text forms into the shape of an arc. The arcs are formed from the top of the text.

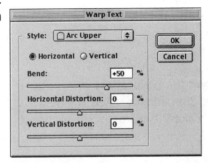

Horizontal
Bend 75

Horizontal
Bend - 75

Horizontal
Bend 75
Horizontal Distortion 75
Vertical Distortion - 50

Vertical
Horizontal Distortion - 75
Horizontal Distortion 75
Vertical Distortion 50

Arch: The text forms an arch – both the top and the bottom line of the text follow the arc.

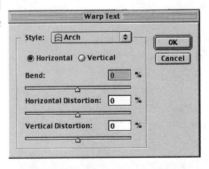

Horizontal
Bend 75

Horizontal
Bend - 75

Horizontal
Bend 75
Horizontal Distortion 75
Vertical Distortion - 50

Vertical
Horizontal Distortion - 75
Horizontal Distortion 75
Vertical Distortion 50

Bulge: The text bulges – the top and bottom line of the text mirror each other.

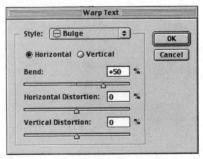

Horizontal
Bend 75

Horizontal
Bend - 75

Horizontal
Bend 75
Horizontal Distortion 75
Vertical Distortion - 50

Vertical
Horizontal Distortion - 75
Horizontal Distortion 75
Vertical Distortion 50

Shell Lower: The bottom line of the text bulges downwards (horizontal), or sideways to the right (vertical). The top line stays constant.

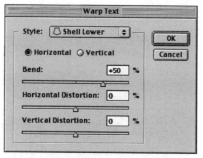

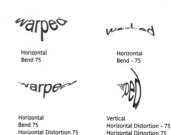

Horizontal
Bend 75

Horizontal
Bend - 75

Horizontal
Bend 75
Horizontal Distortion 75
Vertical Distortion - 50

Vertical
Horizontal Distortion - 75
Horizontal Distortion 75
Vertical Distortion 50

Shell Upper: The top line of the text bulges upwards (horizontal), or sideways to the left (vertical). The bottom line stays constant.

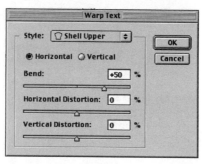

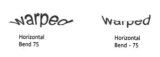

Horizontal
Bend 75

Horizontal
Bend - 75

Horizontal
Bend 75
Horizontal Distortion 75
Vertical Distortion - 50

Vertical
Horizontal Distortion - 75
Horizontal Distortion 75
Vertical Distortion 50

Flag: The text (both its top line and bottom line) follow the line of a flying flag. The higher the bend value, the more undulations in the flag shape. The height of the letters stays constant.

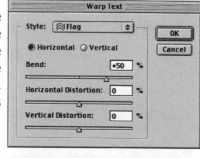

Horizontal
Bend 75

Horizontal
Bend - 75

Horizontal
Bend 75
Horizontal Distortion 75
Vertical Distortion - 50

Vertical
Horizontal Distortion - 75
Horizontal Distortion 75
Vertical Distortion 50

Wave: This is very similar to flag, but where the top and bottom lines of the text and top go downwards they get slightly closer together (the letters are slightly squashed) and where the top and bottom lines go up, they get slightly further apart (the letters are stretched).

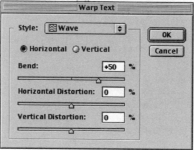

Horizontal
Bend 75

Horizontal
Bend - 75

Horizontal
Bend 75
Horizontal Distortion 75
Vertical Distortion - 50

Vertical
Horizontal Distortion - 75
Horizontal Distortion 75
Vertical Distortion 50

Fish: Text forms the shape of a fish – the bottom and top line of the text come together (letters are squashed) two thirds along the selected text.

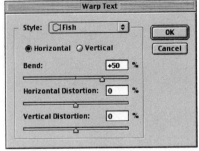

Rise: The text climbs upwards – both the bottom and top line of the text rise. The height of the text stays constant.

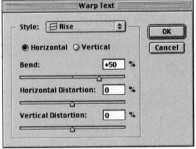
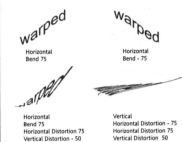

Fisheye: The text looks as though it is being viewed with a fish eye lens. The text curves backwards. The height of the letters stays constant.

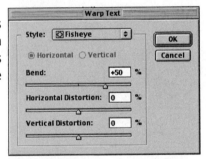
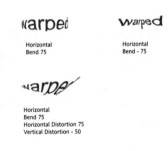

Inflate: The text looks as though it is swelling from the center. The height of the letters becomes greater in the middle.

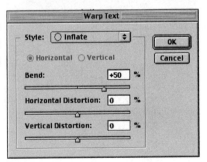

Squeeze: The text is squeezed horizontally at the centerline – the width of the letters becomes smaller at the centerline.

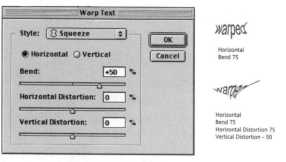

Twist: The text is twisted – the angle of the letters and baseline change, as does the height.

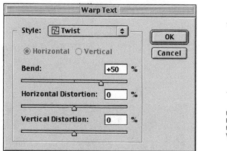

Changing the Opacity of Text

To change the opacity of your text layer (how see-through the text is), select the layer in the Layers palette, then either enter an opacity percentage in the Opacity box (in the top right hand corner of the palette) or use the slider.

The higher the opacity level, the more opaque the text (the less transparent it is).

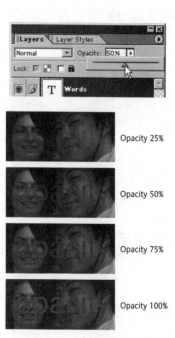

Opacity 25%

Opacity 50%

Opacity 75%

Opacity 100%

Changing the Blending Mode of the Text

The blending mode decides how the text layer interacts with other layers – how the text blends with the image pixels in the lower layers. It is often hard to predict how changing the mode of a text layer will affect the lower layers, as it depends on the hue and saturation of both the text and pixels on lower layers. The best way to learn about how a blending mode will affect the image is to experiment.

To change the blending mode of a text layer, select the layer in the Layer palette and then select a mode from the drop down menu

the top left of the layer palette. For more information, see the previous chapter on layers.

> TIP: Blending modes are fully explained and illustrated in Chapter 3

Rasterize Text

As it has been explained already in this chapter, text layers are vector based, which means they can be edited and transformed without there being any loss of quality in the text. Although this is greatly beneficial in many ways, it does mean that no hue or tone adjustments can be made and that no filters can be applied.

A way to overcome this is to **rasterize** the text. Rasterizing converts vectors to bitmaps. To rasterize a text layer, select it in the Layers palette and go to **Simplify Layer**....

The text will not seem to change in the image window, but in the Layers palette it will change from a text layer to a normal layer.

The text will convert to image pixels and the rest of the layer will become transparent (displayed as gray and white squares in the layer palette). Now it is possible to make hue and tone adjustments and apply filters to the text. It is however no longer possible to edit the text.

> *TIP: See Chapter 7 to learn more about Filters and Chapter 6 to learn more about adjusting hue and tone.*

Applying Effects

As text sits on a layer, it is possible to apply layer styles to it. Styles are a combination of effects that are applied to a layer (which in this case contains text). Photoshop has a large selection of preset styles in the Layer Styles palette.

1. To apply a style to a text layer, select the text layer in the Layers palette.

2. Open the Layer Styles palette.

3. Select a style that you like – some of the more colorful presets are located in the 'Complex' page.

4. To make final touches to the style, click back to the Layers palette and double-click on the round 'f' logo to the right of the text layer.

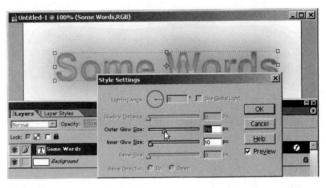

5. Make any final changes you like, then click OK.

> TIP: Layer Styles have been fully explained and illustrated in Chapter 3.

Creating Shadowy text

As you experiment with using text in Photoshop and try combining transformations, warping effects, opacity levels, blending modes and layer styles, you will no doubt come across some results that you will reuse time and time again. One of my favorite combinations I have called Shadowy text. To create shadowy text:

1. Create a text layer by selecting the Text tool and writing in the Image window.

Shadowy Text

2. Duplicate the layer by selecting the text layer in the Layers palette and selecting Duplicate Layer from the Layers palette menu.

3. Flip the duplicated layer selecting it in the Layers palette, then clicking **Image > Rotate > Flip Vertical.** Move the Flipped layer down a little.

Shadowy Text

4. With the duplicated text layer still selected, select the Text tool and click the Warp Text button in the Text Options bar

5. Choose Shell Upper from the Warp Text menu. Adjust the Bend to a value between 30 and 50, and Vertical Distortion settings to a value between -10 and -50.

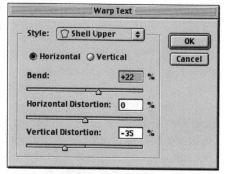

6. Resize the duplicated Text layer to match the original layer (select the layer in the Layers palette, select **Image > Transform > Free Transform** and use the handles).

7. Simplify the text layer using the Menu button in the Layers palette.

8. Now select the text (if you can't remember how, follow these steps).

   ● Select the Magic Wand tool.

   ● Uncheck the Contiguous box at the top of the screen.

   ● Click select in one of the letters in our 'shadow'.

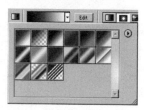

9. Using the Gradient tool, select an appropriate gradation (black to white) and apply a graduated fill (explained in the Chapter 1). If our selection worked, it will only affect the lower letters as they were on their own layer.

10. If you like, change the opacity of the duplicated Text Layer opacity to around 40%, and voila!

Creating Text Outlines

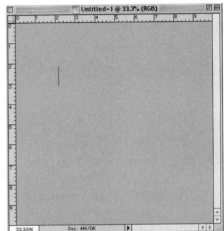

Create Mask or Selection

Rather than typing text that appears as filled vector objects, as we have done so far in this chapter, it is possible to write text that is a mask or selection. This can be very useful if you want your text to be filled with an image rather than a solid color or a style.

To create a mask or selection in the shape of text, select the Text tool. Before clicking in the Image window, look at the text tool options bar. To the left of the options bar are two icons. The first allows you to create a text layer (which we have been doing), the second allows you to create a mask or selection.

1. Click on the Create Selection button and click in the Image window. It will turn pink (unless the settings have been altered).

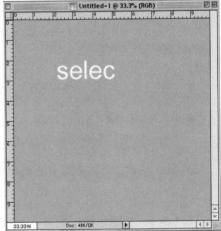

2. When you start to type it will appear in white.

3. When you have finished writing, commit the text by clicking the checkmark icon. No text layer is created, but the text that you entered is converted into a selection marquee (black and white flashing lines).

4. Now that the text exists as a selection it can be stroked or pasted into:

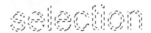

- **Stroking the text selection** will outline it with a color. To do this, Control click the selection and select Stroke from the drop down menu. This will cause a menu to launch, allowing you to select the color and width of the outline and whether the line should be outside, inside, or centered to the marquee.

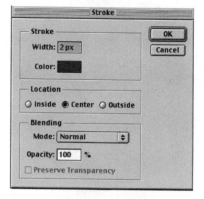

TIP: To learn more about Stroking a selection, (and many other options available with selections) see Chapter 2.

- **Pasting into the text selection** will allow you to fill the text with copied image pixels. To do this, open the file that you want to copy image pixels from, make a selection, and copy the selected pixels. Then return to the file that contains the text selection and go to **Edit > Paste Into**.

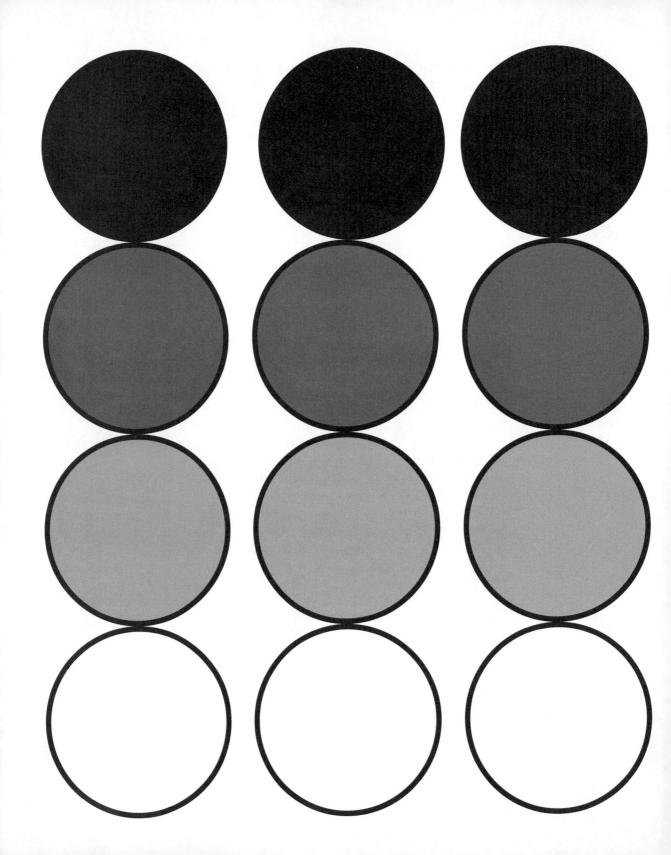

CHAPTER 5
SHAPES

Photoshop Elements combines powerful image (bitmap) editing capabilities with some additional vector abilities. One of these is its ability to handle text, so that it remains editable throughout. Another of these is the Shape tools. For detailed diagram work you are probably still better off with another program, like Illustrator, but it's a good start.

Because these tools are vectors you can produce precise forms; you are not confined by the jaggedness of selecting pixels. These can then be resized without any loss in quality. The paths you draw are also saved independently of the canvas, so you can change the shape later on, and the selection, fill, stroke or form they have helped you produce will change with it.

This can take the way you work to a new level and let you try out ideas without having to keep a finger on the undo button. You won't have to start again if your project requirements change half way through.

The Shape tools in Photoshop Elements are all tucked behind the same icon (whichever was used most recently). By default, they're tucked behind the Custom Shapes tool, set behind a heart, but it can change to reflect the most recently used shape.

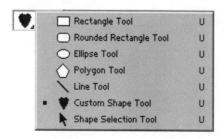

The shapes you draw can remain as shapes, or be converted to traditional pixels, necessary for some effects to be applied. This is called rasterizing.

Drawing Shapes

There are four basic Shape tools (two Rectangle tools – one with rounded corners – the Ellipse tool, and the Polygon tool), a Line tool and the Custom Shapes. Drawing shapes is achieved by clicking and dragging the mouse across the canvas, in the same way as you would create a selection.

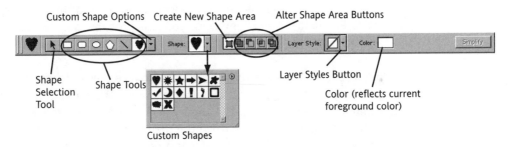

Custom Shape Options   Create New Shape Area   Alter Shape Area Buttons

Shape Selection Tool   Shape Tools   Layer Styles Button   Color (reflects current foreground color)

Custom Shapes

Creating a Custom Shape

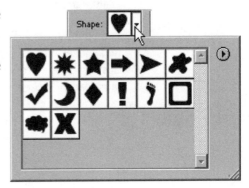

1. Select the Custom Shapes tool from the Toolbox.

2. Select a shape from the Custom Shape picker on the Tool Options bar.

3. Select a color from the Color Picker (accessed towards the right of the Tool Options bar.

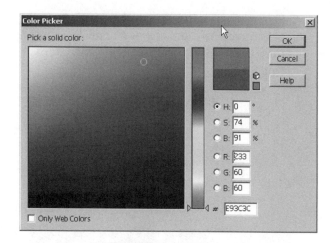

4. Click in the top left of the area you want your shape to appear and drag the pointer down and to the right.

5. When you release the pointer the shape will be colored in.

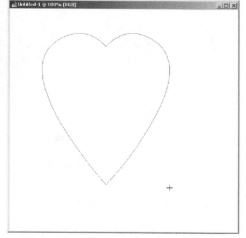

6. Notice that a shape layer has appeared in the Layers palette.

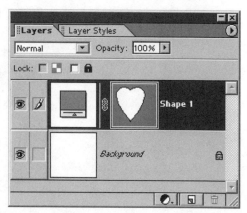

7. Rather than switching to the Layer Styles palette, you can apply styles directly by using the Layer Style button on the Tool Options bar.

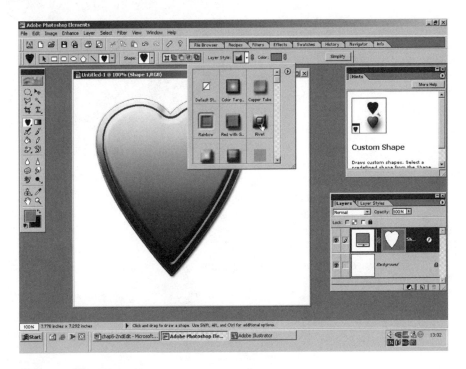

Creating Other Shapes

It is possible to create shapes of your own using the built–in tools.

1. Create a shape using one of the shape tools – Rectangle, Ellipse, or the Custom Shapes tool.

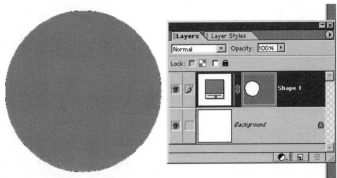

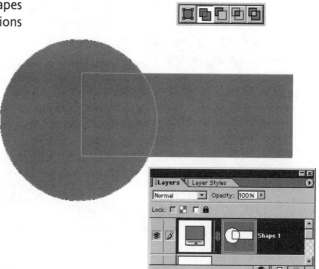

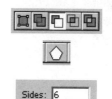

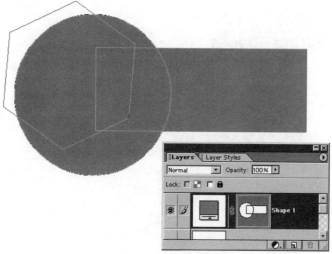

2. Now select the Add To Shapes button from the Tool Options Bar.

3. Select a different shape type from the Tool Options Bar (or the same, if you prefer) and draw it as before.

4. Carrying on in this vein, select the Subtract From Shapes button from the Options bar and then select the Polygon tool.

5. Using the Sides box that appears, increase the number of sides to six (by clicking inside it and typing 6.)

6. Click at the centre of your new polygon and drag to the edge of your new shape.

7. Select a Layer Style if you wish. It will be applied to you whole shape, even though you can still see the bisecting shapes that make up your creation.

8. Beginning to edit a different layer of your artwork will hide the guide lines.

Editing Shapes

While we are working with shapes, it is still possible to go back and correct mistakes we have made. Continuing from the previous example:

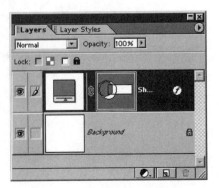

1. Reselect the shape layer by clicking on it in the Layers palette.

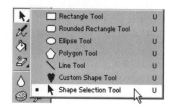

2. Select the Shape Selection tool from the Toolbox or right most of the buttons on the Shape Tool Options Bar.

3. Now click on one of the shapes in the layer. If you click on an area with more than one shape, the most recent (uppermost) will be selected.

4. You can now drag the selected shape to a new position on the shape layer.

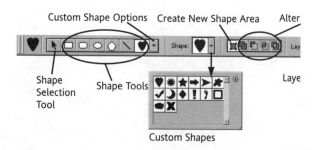

5. You can also alter the Add/Subtract/Intersect/Exclude options by clicking on one of these buttons while the shape is still selected.

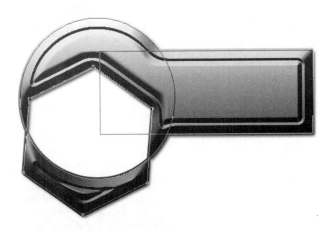

6. If you're still not happy with a part of the shape layer, then you can delete it by pressing the delete or backspace key on your keyboard.

Simplifying the Layer

Some tools and commands, like painting and filters, cannot be applied to shapes, which are vectors. They have to be rasterized. Select the layer and choose Layer > Simplify.

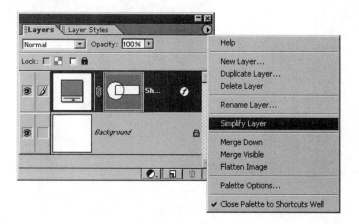

The layer, including any layer styles applied to it, will be converted to pixels, and the individual shapes will no longer be editable.

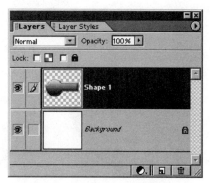

TIP: To make it easier to edit layer styles, it might be easier to apply them after simplifying the shape layer.

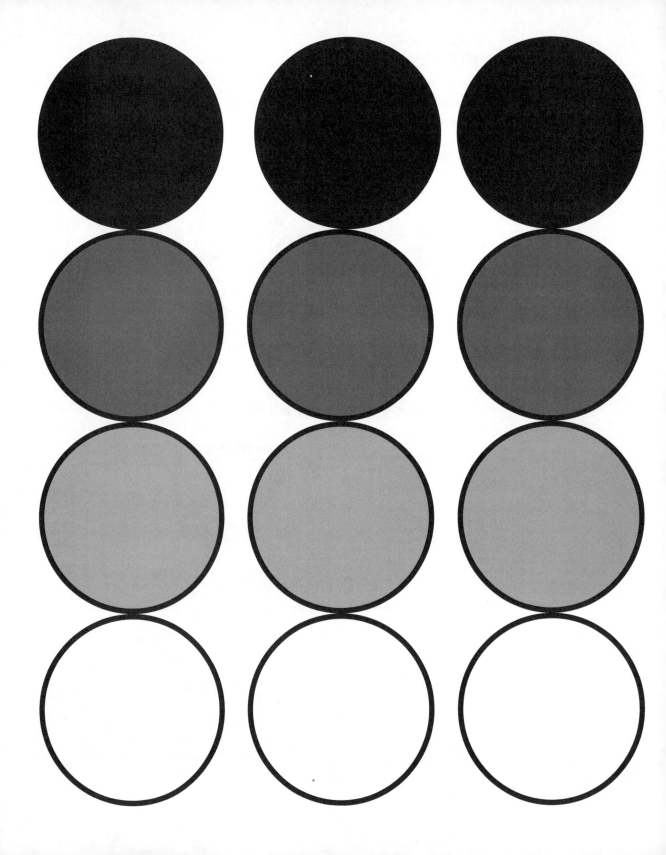

CHAPTER 6
IMAGE
CORRECTION

When a scanned image is opened in Photoshop, you may find that the colors are not as they should be: that in the process of scanning some of the colors have been changed. Alternatively, it may have been the colors in the original that looked wrong. Whatever the reason, you will often come across images that you want to make color adjustments to.

Fortunately, Photoshop gives us a whole menu to help us to correct the color in our images. Some of the options do a lot of the work for us; others give us an high degree of control. Some options are designed to tackle tonal problems, others the hues (colors), and some affect both tones and hues. To decide which of the options we should use, we first need to understand the kind of image that we are working with, and what we are doing to our images when we adjust their colors.

Grayscale – Images made of 256 shades of grey. The only color adjustment options available to use with grayscale images are those that tackle tonal problems.

RGB – Images made of Red, Green and Blue. RGB are known as **additive** colors. When Red, Green and Blue are present at their full strength, they make white; when they are at their lowest values they make black.

RGB is how color is created in the real world. Sunlight is made of full strength RGB light. The reason we see so many other colors is because different colored objects absorb different amounts of RGB. When the sun shines onto a green object, for example, it absorbs the red and blue light and reflects the green light, so the eye perceives it as green.

RGB is also how a computer monitor displays images. There are three lights inside a monitor that shine different intensities of red, green and blue light. When these are mixed, they create all the colors that are available on a color monitor.

In the following pages, we will learn about all the different color adjustment options and find out which is the best option to solve any color problems in our images. Which of the options you choose depends largely on how much you need to understand about the changes. If you need to make very precise changes in order to correct the colors of a print you will want to use an option that gives use a lot of control. If you just want the image to look good for your monitor however, you will not need to spend so much time and effort and therefore choose one of the more direct, intuitive options.

> TIP: Different monitors will display images slightly differently due to color temperatures in the monitor. There is no 100% cure for this problem but calibrating your monitor and doing color print tests can help.

Brightness/Contrast

First let us look at the Brightness/Contrast option. As its name suggests, it allows us to alter the brightness and contrast within our image. The Brightness/Contrast window allows us to make our images brighter or darker and to adjust the contrast by using the sliders or entering positive or negative values.

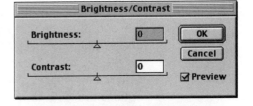

In the example shown the image was far too dark, especially around the figure who is in the shade. By increasing the Brightness to +50, and the Contrast to +20, we are able to see more of the figure but still keep a strong black. We do however lose all the detail in the light areas.

Using Brightness / Contrast is a quick and intuitive way to correct the tonal range of an image. It does however tend to lead us to losing either the midrange or the extreme whites/blacks.

Levels

An alternative to Brightness and Contrast is Levels. In Photoshop Elements, the levels option allows us to look at a histogram which tells us where in the color range the colors in the image are. For example, an image with high contrast will appear to have peaks at either end as much of it is either dark or light.

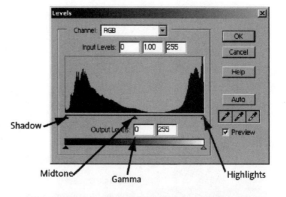

Applying Levels to Grayscale Images

Shadow

Midtone   Gamma   Highlights

1. Open an image saved in grayscale.

2. Click Enhance > Brightness/Contrast > Levels....

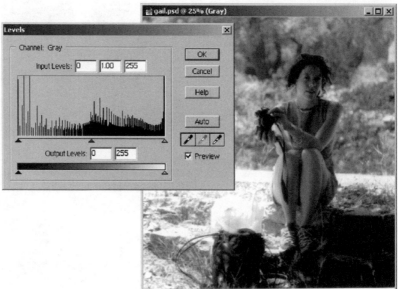

3. Try clicking and dragging on the sliders below the histogram. First drag the marker on the right in a bit.

4. Drag it back and then try dragging the Shadows (dark tones) marker in from the left. By experimenting with the sliders, you can set a tonal range to suit you.

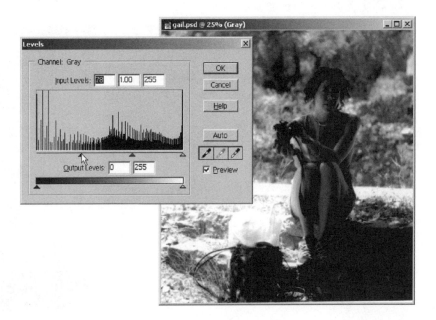

5. You can also adjust the midtone slider. Moving the midtone slider to the right makes the middle range lighter and to the left, makes the midtone darker.

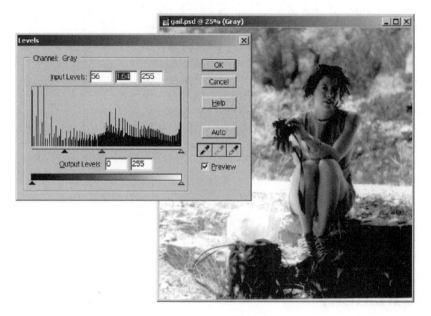

For this image, the best option was to move the midtone point over to the right. This worked better than the Brightness/Contrast option as it allowed me to lighten the image, but still maintain nice shadows.

Applying Color to Color Images

When correcting color images using levels it is possible not only to change the overall tonal range of the image, but also the tonal range in each of the individual color channels, Red, Green and Blue. When working with an RGB image for example, it is also possible to change the balance of shadows, midtones and highlights in just the reds, the blues or the greens. To select a channel, choose it from the Channel drop down menu.

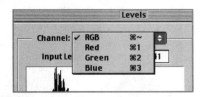

Variations

Using Variations is the easiest and most visual way to control color adjustment in your image but definitely not the most powerful. The Variations window gives you thumbnails of how adding red, green blue magenta etc. will affect your image.

In addition, it allows you to specify whether you are adding color to the shadows, midtones or highlights, and to adjust the intensity of the color change. Variations is a good tool if you are new to color or if you need to refresh your memory as to how adding certain colors will affect an image.

1. Load an image that needs to be color corrected.

2. Click Enhance > Variations….

3. You can adjust your image (represented by the centre thumbnail) by clicking on any of the others around it. Once you have clicked once, the centre image changes to reflect your change.

Compare your current pick to the original

Select to affect the Shadows Midtones, Highlights or Saturation

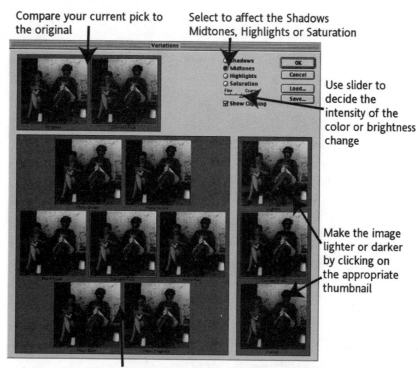

Use slider to decide the intensity of the color or brightness change

Make the image lighter or darker by clicking on the appropriate thumbnail

Make the image more red, green, blue, cyan, magenta or yellow by clicking on the appropriate thumbnail

4. To see what parts of the image are being affected, check the Show Clipping box.

5. You can continue changing steps (the original will always appear in the top left) until you click OK.

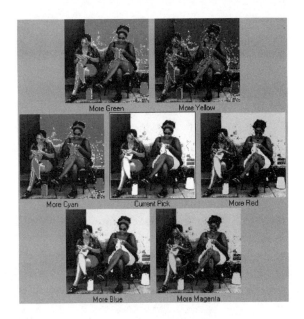

Hue/Saturation

Hue/Saturation works on the Hue (color), Saturation (intensity) and Lightness (tone) of the image. Hue/Saturation is great for making big color shifts in your image. At the bottom of the window are two color spectrum bars, the top one shows us the original, the lower, the new spectrum (color shift) in the image.

The Hue Slider allows you to shift the color range in the image (or a channel). We can either make the whole of our image more cyan (selecting Master from the Channel drop down menu) or make just the Reds more cyan (by selecting Red from the drop down menu). The **Saturation** and **Lightness** sliders then control the intensity and the brightness of the cyan.

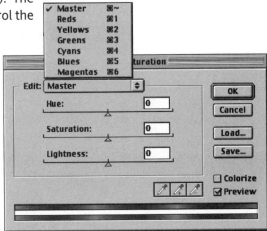

Making Alien Faces

One fun use of this tool is to recolor part of an image – say someone's face – by selecting it before applying the color:

1. Select the areas of your image to be affected – the Magic Wand tool is handy here.

2. Feather your selection (softening the edges) by clicking Select > Feather and choosing a small radius.

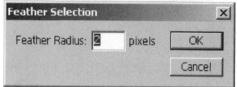

3. Select Enhance > Color > Hue/Saturation….

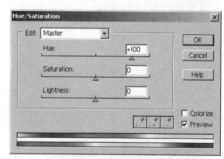

4. Drag the Hue slider to a value of about 100.

5. Deselect the selection. You should be left with some nice green alien skin (you'll just have to try it yourself, or take our word for it!).

Making a Sepia Tone

You can also make changes to your whole images, to create a sepia tone for example:

1. Open the color image that you want to want to work with.

2. Open the Hue/Saturation box as before.

3. Check the Colorize box so that your color change correctly affects all the colors in the image.

4. Adjust the Hue slider to 34.

5. When you have achieved the right hue click OK.

   You will have noticed as you were moving the slider that many other tones can also be achieved too.

Replacing Color

Another option is the Replace Color tool:

1. Open the image you wish to alter.

2. Click Enhance > Color > Replace Color....

3. To select the color that we want to change, we use the Eyedropper to select a pixel from the Image window and the selection is previewed in the Replace Color window.

4. Add other colors to the selection by using the plus eyedropper, and take colors out of the selection by using the minus eyedropper.

5. The **Fuzziness** slider which acts like Tolerance allows us to decide how many similarly colored pixels are included in the selection. Once a selection has been made, we can then change its color.

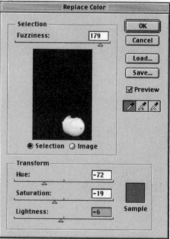

6. At the bottom of the window there are sliders for Hue, Saturation and Brightness, use the Hue slider to select a color, and then the Saturation and brightness sliders to select its saturation and brightness. Make sure the preview box is checked so that you can see the changes in the image window. When you are satisfied with the change click OK.

Dodge and Burn Tools

Sometimes in an image it is only a certain area that is too dark or too light. The Dodge and Burn tools can be used to correct these areas. The terms Dodge and Burn come from traditional photography. In photography, when we 'dodge' an area we give it less light than the rest of the image in order to stop it getting too dark, whilst when we 'burn' an area, we give it more light to make it darker.

In Photoshop, the Dodge and Burn tools act like brushes that darken or lighten areas. Via the Dodge/Burn tool Options bar, we can specify the size of the brush, whether the tool affects the shadows, midtones or highlights. We can also specify the strength of the tool (Exposure).

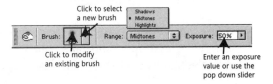

In the example the woman's face is in shadow. To rectify this we can use the Dodge tool.

In this example, which is color photocopy of an old photograph, due to reproduction, the central area of the image has been bleached and definition has been lost in the mans face and on the label of the bottles. By using the Burn tool we can bring out the details without affecting the rest of the picture.

Replacing the Sky

Often we may have a photograph of a place or a person, but feel the sky behind them is so dull that it doesn't do the subject justice. Changing the sky can add drama or atmosphere to an image. Replacing the sky in a Photoshop image can be easily done using the Selection tools and then a little cut-and-pasting.

Let's start by looking at a photograph of Rome. The ruins are stunning but unfortunately the sky is very white and flat.

Fortunately, I also have a photograph that was taken off the shores of Tenerife as the sun was setting.

The sky and clouds are a burnt orange red. How great it would be to place this dramatic sky into my photograph of Rome. Well, with a few easy steps in Photoshop, we can!

1. The first step is to select the sky that needs to be replaced. In this example it is the white sky in Rome.

Select the sky using the Magic Wand tool.

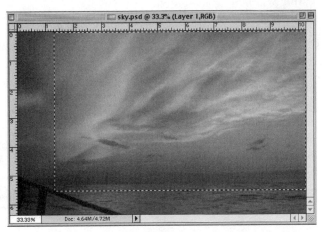

2. Once the sky has been selected, the file that contains the sky that is going to be placed into the image needs to be opened. Once open, select the sky, either by selecting the entire image; Ctrl/⌘-A, or by drawing a marquee and then copying the sky; Edit > Copy or Ctrl/⌘-C.

3. Now, we can return to the original image and paste the sky into the selection (Edit > Paste Into or Ctrl/⌘-Shift-V). The sky will now be pasted into the selection and a new layer will be created in the layer window. By pasting pixels into a selection, Photoshop automatically converts the selection into a mask.

4. Finally in order to uniform the whole image, you may want to adjust the color temperature of the foreground to suit the sky. In the example, the foreground now needs to be made warmer. To do this use the Variations tool.

Image Dirt and the Clone Tool

When scanning an image, you often pick up some image dirt, particularly when scanning in slides. In most cases, cleaning the scanner and the original, and then scanning again can rectify this. However, if the dirt is not in/on the scanner but part of the image (or if we no longer have access to a scanner), we will have to clean up the image in Photoshop. This is can be done using the Clone tool.

The Clone tool works by cloning (copying) an area of pixels and then pasting them into another area. Although it sounds like the Clone tool is just another way of copying and pasting (which in essence it is) it can be refined via the Options bar to work like a paintbrush at various opacities, in various blending modes and in an aligned or non aligned mode.

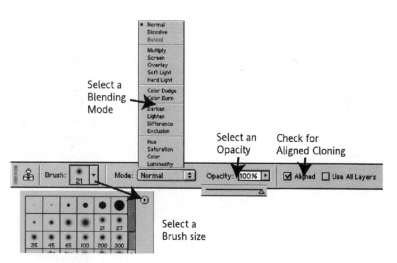

When using the Clone tool we first have to select the clone source (the place we are cloning pixels from). It is possible to either ask the source to stay in the same place (**non aligned**) or for the source to follow the brush (**aligned**). If we choose the Aligned option the first two clicks we make – the click to select the source and then the click to start painting with the cloned pixels, decides the angle and distance of the clone source to the brush. When we paint with the Clone tool, the clone source turns into a cross.

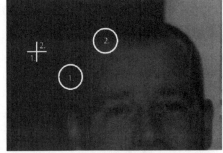

Non - Aligned the source stays in the same place

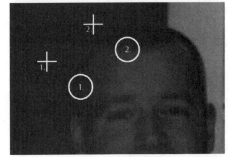

Aligned the source moves with the brush

1. To use the Clone tool on an image, select it from the Toolbox.

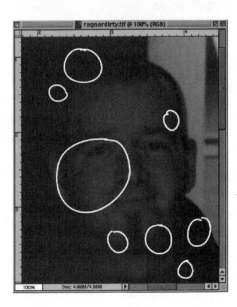

TIP: Be careful to select the Clone tool and not the Pattern tool – they look very alike but selecting the wrong can drive you crazy!

Find the area of your image that you want to clean up. In the example there are a number of areas of image dirt. I shall clean up the face. There are a number of specks of dust, plus a horrible hair that need to be cloned out.

2. First, let's clone out the spots of dust. Spots of dust appear as white pixels on your image.

3. Zoom in close to the spot of dust and move the Clone tool near the dust. The icon for the Clone tool will be a circle that indicates the size of the brush you are using. In the example the size of the brush is too big for the area that we need to clone.

4. To make the brush smaller, select a smaller brush from the **Brush** drop down menu in the Options bar or modify the existing brush by making the diameter smaller.

5. Once your brush is the correct size (it should be just a bit bigger then the spot of dust that you want to clone out), find an area of pixels near the spot of dust that are the right color to cover the dust convincingly. In the example I have chosen to clone the area of pixels just above the dust.

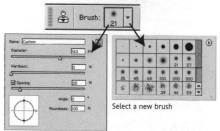

Modify an existing brush · Select a new brush

6. Alt-Click this spot to make it the source of the cloning. When you press down the Alt key, notice that the cursor changes to the Clone Icon.

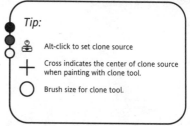

Tip:

Alt-click to set clone source

Cross indicates the center of clone source when painting with clone tool.

Brush size for clone tool.

7. Now move the cursor (which has changed back to the brush icon) and click. The Clone tool will cover the spot with the pixels that were cloned before. Keep clicking until the dust has gone.

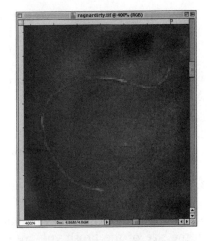

Now let us now move to a more tricky area – the hair across the face.

In this example the hair traverses a number of different tones and colors. We will therefore need to work in Aligned Clone mode (check the Align box in the Tool Options Bar). Zoom in very close to the area so that we are sure of the pixels we are cloning and select a very small brush. Also, take the opacity down to about 80% so that we can work slowly and build up the covering pixels.

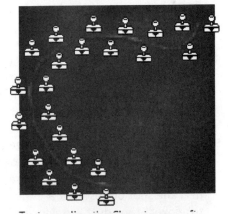

Clone an area as close to the hair as possible. Although it is possible to click and drag across the area that we want to clone out, I suggest continuing to dab / click to clone out the area to give as much control as possible. It will be necessary to re-align the tool often in this example as the tones across the face change so much and because the angle of the hair changes.

8. In the example I re-aligned the Clone tool every 4 or 5 clicks to either side of the hair so that pixels from both sides would build to cover the hair evenly (I kept the opacity down all the time).

Red Eye Removal

Red eyes are a common problem with modern cameras, and can make perfectly innocent people look a little demonic. The problem is caused by the light of the camera's flash being reflected by the pupil of the eye. Many cameras compensate for this by a feature called red eye reduction, which attempts to reduce the size of the pupil – a natural reaction - by flashing a light at the subject before the final photo is taken.

Not only is the effect slightly annoying but it slows down the process of taking the photo, draws more power and very rarely seems to work. It even causes the subject to screw up their eyes most of the time.

The best way to reduce the effect is to fire the flash off another surface – say the ceiling – or if possible move the flash further from the lens so the reflected light isn't aimed straight back. However, if you've got photos with the problem, Photoshop Elements has a handy tool to remove them with a couple of clicks.

1. Open your damaged image (or scan it at as high a resolution as possible).

2. Select the Zoom tool and magnify the area with the affected eyes.

3. Now select the Red Eye Brush tool from the Toolbox.

4. The Tool Options bar changes, notice how at the far left end there is a Brush button, and that there are two colors, the Current, which reflects the color under the mouse pointer, and the replacement, which defaults to black.

5. Move the pointer over the eye. The circle should surround the whole red area. If it does not, select a larger brush using the Brush button on the Tool Options bar.

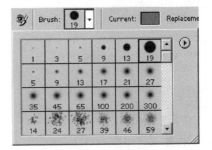

6. Once you are happy with the brush size, click once at the centre of the red area.

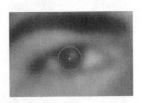

7. There is no need to use red as a replacement color (or, indeed, to replace a red color). If you like, select another color by clicking on the replacement color in the Tool Options bar. If you click on the default button it will return to black.

8. Click on the eye or area to change color in the same way.

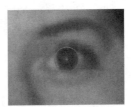

Our final picture gives the chap in the centre dark eyes, and the chap on the right bright blue ones.

The Red Eye Brush tool need not be used simply by clicking once, as we have done. If you click and hold you can use it like any other brush in Photoshop to replace whole areas of color while maintaining the texture below.

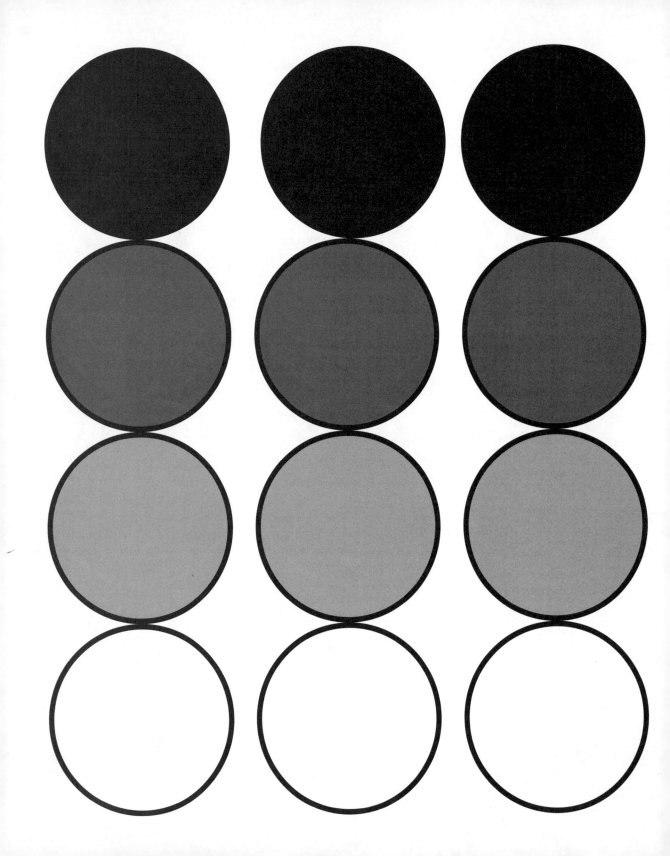

CHAPTER 7
SPECIAL EFFECTS

The special effects that Photoshop is capable of are often the first thing that people think of when Photoshop is mentioned. Someone who uses it as part of their professional life may only use one or two filters regularly, but they remain the most visually impressive thing the program can do and so this chapter is devoted to them.

As we will see these tools give you the license to perform all sorts of distortion and trickery. When Photoshop first came out all these effects were new and exciting – designers applied them to anything just for the sake of it.

The results can look horrible, man-made, and gratuitous; they can make the image look cheap, and end up having the opposite effect to that you had intended. Filters can improve a good image but they will never make a bad photo any better.

If you apply caution and plan what you are trying to get across when using filters you will end up with a more professional looking image. Never let the effect become the focus of the image. There is nothing worse than a large effect applied for no reason.

The Impressionist Brush

The Impressionist brush creates the effect that an area of your image has been stroked by an artists brush. It can be quite useful for picking out the centre of an image.

1. Open the image you wish to alter.

2. Select the Impressionist Brush tool from the toolbox.

3. Select the size and type of brush stroke you want using the Tool Options Bar.

TIP: Experience suggests that a smaller size and an uncomplicated brush is probably most effective with this tool.

4. Select the style you would prefer. There are a number of different stroke effects possible.

5. Stroke over your image in areas where you can afford to loose the detail. Remember the undo tool is always there.

Style: Loose Curl

Tight Short
Tight Medium
Tight Long
Loose Medium
Loose Long
Dab
Tight Curl
Tight Curl Long
Loose Curl
Loose Curl Long

Liquify

This is a fun tool which borrows effects from SuperGoo, a plug-in that has become popular over the years. With its tools you can move, bloat, warp, pucker and twirl, distorting parts of an image, as if you are moving thick wet paint around a canvas. These effects really come into their own for making fun of friends and family.

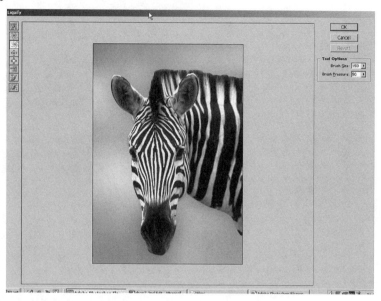

Using Liquify

Liquify brings up a full size window that gives you real-time previews. The changes aren't made permanent until you click the OK button (at the top right corner of the liquify window) and return to Photoshop.

The Liquify window shows your image full size. The tools are listed on the left and the brush, reconstructing, freezing and viewing options on your right-hand side.

To apply an effect click or drag across the image. Using the tool options on the top right, change the brush size and pressure to control the rate and harshness that you distort the image.

— Warp
— Twirl clockwise
— Twirl anti-clockwise
— Pucker
— Bloat
— Shift pixels
— Reflection
— Reconstruct

Warp

The Warp tool pushes pixels in the direction you drag the brush.

This is my original image. A pretty zebra you'll agree.

Dragging from the bottom left knocks the poor guy sideways...

...but dragging from the top with a smaller brush head and more controlled strokes can turn this zebra into a giraffe.

Twirling

This does exactly what it suggests. It takes all the pixels inside the brush area and twirls them clockwise or anti-clockwise as if they were on a disc. The longer the button is held, the more the effect...

...this turns his coat psychedelic

Pucker and Bloat

Pucker sucks pixels in towards the center of the brush head, and Bloat pushes them out to the edge. The movement continues as long as you have the brush held down.

Turn him into an anteater...

...or give him x-ray vision.

Shift pixels

The Shift tool moves pixels at right angles to the direction you drag in.

I dragged the brush up from the center bottom.

By default the pixels move to the left, but hold down the Alt key while you drag and they move to the right.

Reflection

The Reflection tool copies pixels from the right of your brush. The pixels are picked from the right on an upward stroke and the left on the way down.

Using Ctrl/⌘, I dragged from the left to create a hammerhead.

Resetting

Click the Revert button on the left to reset the image, or use the Reconstruct tool to gradually massage a specific area back to its original state. While you hold the brush down, the pixels are drawn back to the centre. Sadly, however, there is no step-by-step history while you're using this tool, you either revert to the start or carry on.

The Filters Palette

The filters are grouped and can be found in the Filters palette, or the filter menu. They are Photoshop's main tools for performing a whole range of special effects. They work by mathematically rearranging the pixels using formulae that examine the surrounding pixels.

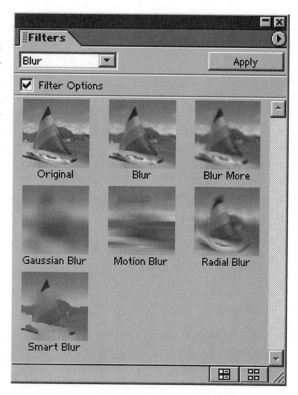

There are many filters that come with Photoshop and hundreds more can be added as plugins from other companies. They can drastically affect the way your photo looks, from a subtle motion blur to adding clouds.

TIP: For a smoother transition between the filtered areas, apply the feather before selecting.

Applying a filter

1. Open an image and, if you wish, select an area to apply the filter to.

2. Click on the Filters palette – it's often easier to use it directly from the Palette Well.

3. Select the filter you wish to use – the thumbnails give a good clue as to what effect they will have.

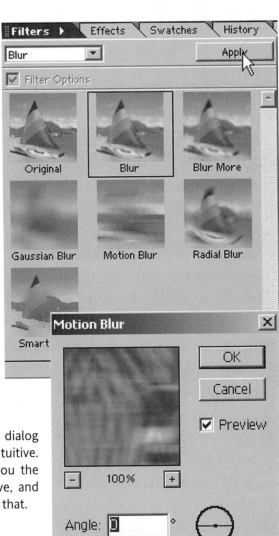

4. Click the Apply filter button.

5. Many filters will bring up an options dialog box. These vary, but are all fairly intuitive. A small area of the image shows you the effect your current settings will have, and any options you have appear below that.

6. Once you have made your changes, click OK and the whole image will be processed.

Some filters take up a huge amount of memory to perform their effects, especially in a high-resolution image. The progress is shown in the bottom left hand corner of the window. To reduce the time taken, select a smaller area; the filter will only apply itself to that area. Or alternatively you could reduce the resolution but the results will appear harsher.

TIP: To maximize the effect of a filter heighten the contrast in the image first.

The Effects

There are around 100 filters included in the filters menu. The main ten categories are shown below:

Artistic

the original image

colored pencil

cutout

dry brush

film grain

fresco

neon glow

paint daubs

palette knife

plastic wrap

poster edges

rough pastels

smudge stick

sponge

underpainting

watercolour

Blur

gaussian blur

motion blur

radial blur

smart blur (normal)

smart blur (edges)

Brush Strokes

accented edges

angled strokes

crosshatch

dark strokes

ink outlines

spatter

sprayed strokes

sumi-e

diffuse glow

glass

ocean ripple

Distort

pinch

polar coordinates

ripple

shear

spherize

twirl

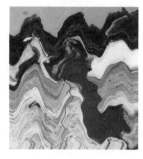

wave

zigzag

Noise

add noise

median

Pixelate

color halftone

crystallize

fragment

mezzotint

mosaic

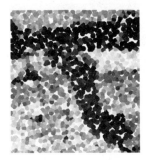

pointillize

Sharpen

sharpen more

unsharp mask

Sketch

bas relief

chalk and charcoal

charcoal

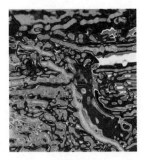

chrome

conte crayon

graphic pen

halftone pattern

notepaper

photocopy

plaster

reticulation

stamp

torn edges

water paper

Stylize

diffuse

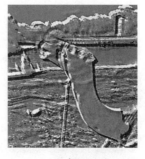

emboss

extrude

155

find edges

glowing edges

solarize

tiles

trace contour

wind

Texture

craquelure

grain (horizontal)

mosaic tiles

patchwork

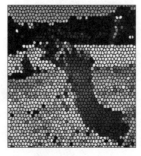

stained glass

texturizer

The Effects Palette

While filters are effectively mathematical in nature, relating each pixel to each other, Photoshop Elements also includes some more dramatic, if less useful or customisable, effects.

They are accessed in much the same way as the filters, from their own palette, which, for the most part, is probably best left in the Palette Well.

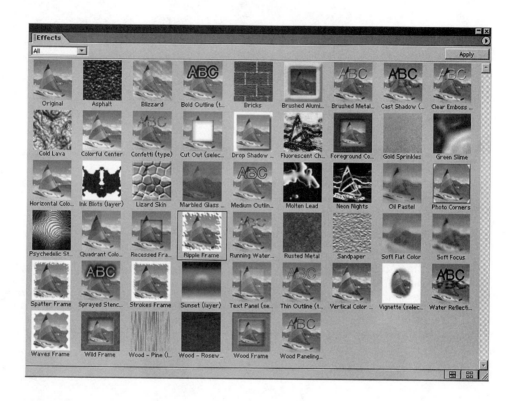

1. Select the image you wish to apply the effect to. Some may not work on selections.

2. Click Apply.

3. Some of the effects take a few moments to apply – they are often a combination of other effects, so the percentage chart in the bottom left hand side of the screen may need to repeat its cycle a number of times.

Photomerge

If you have a series of photographs taken in a row, you can merge them using Photomerge to create a panoramic image, a cheap alternative to a wide-angled lens.

1. Ensure you know where all your source images are saved. In this example we're using some hand-held snaps taken in less than ideal conditions, but clearly images taken with a tripod would help the computer greatly.

2. Open Photoshop Elements and click File > Photomerge....

3. Click the Add... button, which will bring up a dialog allowing you to select the images you are going to use.

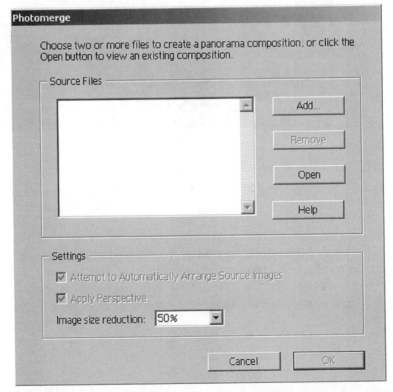

4. Holding Shift allows you to click on more than one image before pressing Open.

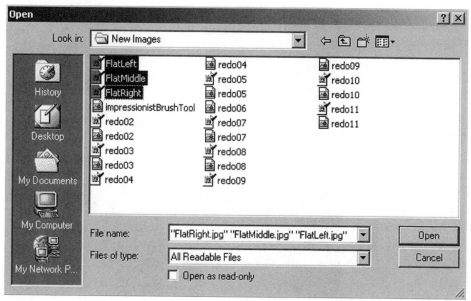

5. Once you are satisfied with the list of images in your Source Files window, select "Attempt to automatically arrange..." at the bottom and then OK.

6. Unless your images are very clearly defined the computer may have trouble identifying the overlaps. In which case, you have to give it a hand. After a few seconds of trying, you may see this message.

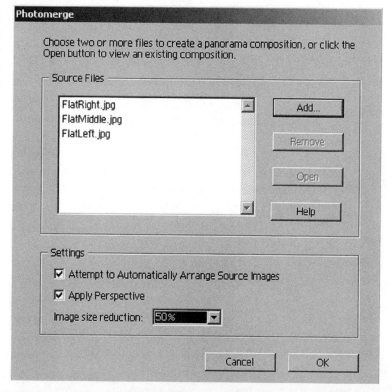

7. A large window will appear with small thumbnails of your images at the top.

8. Drag one of the thumbnails out to the main work area, perhaps the centre one, and then drag the second out and try and line it up with the first.

9. If you have trouble lining it up with the other shapes, it may help to adjust the zoom level with the slider to the right.

10. You can also rotate any of your images to help align them by selecting the Rotate tool (see right) and clicking and dragging inside one of the images.

11. Once you're happy with the rotation of your image, drag it to line up with the next. The computer will attempt to line them up again, but probably with more success.

12. Repeat these steps for all your images. You may find it helps to set a vanishing point. Do so by selecting 'Use Perspective' on the right of the window, then selecting the Set Vanishing Point tool (see right) and clicking on the vanishing point.

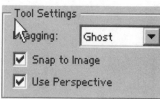

13. When you're happy click OK and the machine will tidy everything up to produce the final result. You may need to use Photoshop's other tools to tidy up some of the edges.

CHAPTER 8
OUTPUT

Once you've imported your image and altered it in any way you want, it is time to get it out to your audience. In this chapter we look at two basic methods, printing your image and putting it on the Internet.

The only word of warning is that both of these methods, in one way or another, depend on things outside Photoshop. Your printer will come with its own software, which isn't always the same, and, while web pages look the same, the way they are copied from your machine to the internet depends on your service provider.

Paper Output

Printing in Photoshop Elements, much like in other applications, depends greatly upon your own printer. To get the best possible output, read the documentation that came with your printer. If you are using a modern inkjet (like many Epson, Canon or HP machines) you should find that, using good quality special paper, you can produce very good quality prints, if you're prepared to wait for them.

Printing

To make full use of your paper, you'll want to print the image as large as possible.

1. Select the Print Preview button from the Shortcut bar at the top of the screen.

2. In the Print Preview window, your picture will be represented as it would appear on your printer's default paper size.

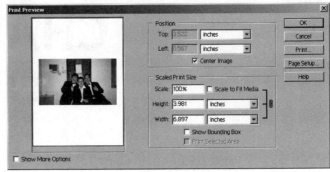

3. To ensure your printer is set to its highest quality settings, click on Page Setup.

4. Select your Printer from the pull down menu at the top, then click the Properties... button.

5. A dialog to adjust the set up of your printer will appear (this varies from machine to machine). Select the highest resolution (or whichever you want). You should also set the mode to landscape if you think that would benefit your image, and set the paper type. (The window you see will probably not look quite the same unless you have an Epson Stylus Photo 890. Different printers come with different software, though terms like landscape and portrait stay the same).

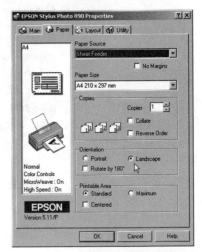

6. Click OK, then OK again in the Page Setup dialogue to return to the Print Preview window.

7. If you want to expand the image from the natural size (set by the resolution) click on the Fit to Page button.

8. When you're happy with the size, click on the Print... button.

9. In the final dialog, set the number of copies you want and click OK. The lower section of the box deals with any color management settings you have, and may not appear at all.

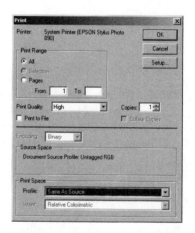

Multiple Copies on the Same Page

Photoshop also includes a quick method to create a whole page with a number of copies of an image, at different sizes. This is a handy way to share photos.

1. Open the image you wish to make multiple copies of.

2. Click **File > Automate > Picture Package**.

3. Check the Use Foreground Document box if it isn't already.

4. Choose your own Layout from the dropdown menu. There are a number of different options, and once you click on one a preview will appear in the bottom right of the dialog.

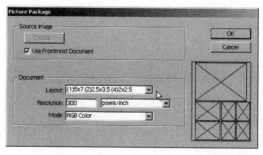

5. Set an appropriate resolution for your printer. 300 dpi is a sensible maximum on an inkjet of 1440 dpi

6. Ensure that the Mode is set to RGB Color if you want to print in color.

7. Click OK. The computer will then spend a little while making copies of your image at the size(s) you have selected. Give it time, it may take a few minutes.

8. You will be presented with a new image file, which you can print as you see fit.

Web Output

Photoshop has always been able to export the various image formats that can be displayed on the web. But the options have been limited and a method of trial and error was always used until the required result was found. Designing for a screen was no problem, but designing for the web is about much more than looks. File size, interaction and technical parameters have to be taken into consideration.

Photoshop Elements includes an export facility that makes it easier to export images for the web. It allows you to see the results of exporting an image before you save the file. Adobe have also brought in the option to select only web-safe colors when creating your work.

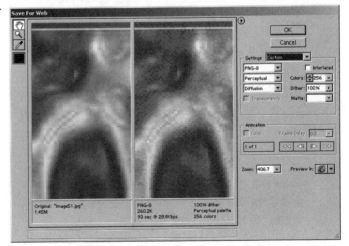

In the rest of this chapter we'll cover the things you need to keep in mind when designing for the web and how you go about preparing these graphics.

Designing for the web

Web sites are put together using a language called HTML, a plain text description of how that page should be displayed when viewed in a browser. It describes how a number of elements should look.

Eight years ago web sites just consisted of text. You could use HTML to describe the color and size of the text, and the color of the background. You could add images, tables and horizontal bars but not much else. This was constrained as much by the speed that the page had to download as by the simplicity of the language. Visually, pages were pretty dull, and not much different to word documents rather than the multimedia environments we know today.

Pages are still constructed using the same simple language, though you can make life even easier these days by saving from a word processor like Microsoft Word.

```
<HTML>
<BODY>
This is a <B>very</B> basic web page
</BODY>
</HTML>
```

As technology improved allowing faster modems, and business moved onto the web, there was a distinct push to make the design quality on a par with traditional mediums like print and television. Because this development environment is pretty basic, images are used to create a title in a nicer, smoother font, create constructive elements to give the page different styles, or to represent real-world objects or environments.

TIP: You can learn more about this if you like at http://www.hitmill.com/internet/web_history.html

Thinking websites

If you're going to design the pages yourself, think about how the page will be constructed. Imagine HTML as scaffolding. How are you going to cut up your images to construct the page around the content and links? You can use tables to split up the page and allow different elements to be placed across the width of the screen, rather than making the user scroll down to see the whole of the page. Effective use of your table could allow you to construct a layout as complex as www.amazon.com or www.bbc.co.uk.

Think about the file size and therefore the download time. Use HTML and the images intelligently to make the file size smaller. HTML will always be most efficient for producing text and large areas of color. In the rest of the chapter, we'll make images as small as possible.

In Photoshop, it also helps to think in layers. Always put each element of your design onto a different layer and save them separately. For example, if you are designing a page with a background, you will need to hide all the foreground elements to save the background. Or you may lay out certain elements that will be rendered in HTML; they may be overlapping other images that you need to save individually.

Think about the screen size the page will fit in. It is good practice to take a screenshot of your browser and design a page within that. The most common screen size is 800x600 pixels, but, with all the usual browser menus, the actual size you have to play with is roughly 780x460. The browsers can obviously scroll downwards, but unless you have masses of content keep the vertical size to within that. If you want impact, the message will be lost if it the user has to find it!

Overall, think the lowest common denominator. Your page could be viewed by millions of people with thousands of different computers, and you want as many people to be able to see your site as possible. Common constraints are:

- The download speed; 56kbps modems are the norm so try to keep your whole page under 50k

- The number of colors; a lot of people can only see 256 colors, so use the web palette if you want to be safe. But this is becoming less and less common, so don't worry about this one too much.

- The screen size; 640x480 used to be the standard size, 800x600 is the norm now.

- Different browsers support different versions of HTML. Although the latest versions incorporate layers and stylesheets, stick to tables to build your pages and you'll be fine.

> ● *TIP: Modem speeds are*
> ● *measured using bits per*
> ○ *second, whereas most*
> *computer measurements*
> *are in bytes (Kb=kilobytes).*
> *A 56K(bits)ps modem, at*
> *theoretical maximum, can*
> *only receive 7K(bytes) a*
> *second, and in reality the*
> *figure is typically nearer*
> *3Kb/sec.*

Optimization

There are a few image formats, like GIF, JPEG or PNG that use clever compression techniques to make images tiny, in comparison to traditional formats like BMP or TIFF. As MP3 has drastically reduced the file size of songs by eliminating the 'noise' that we don't really notice, so these image formats reduce the number of colors, or merge areas together that are masked by a photograph's hazy style.

Only GIF and JPEG formats are currently supported by every browser. They have their own advantages and disadvantages. Let the content of the image determine which format you save in. Use the following guide to decide:

GIF

The GIF is an old 8-bit format, meaning it can only contain a maximum of 256 colors. It's good for areas of flat color, or images with well-defined edges, such as text, or constructive elements like buttons. GIF images are also a very well established standard.

The lower the number of colors the smaller its output size. GIFs can be saved as interlaced versions that appear gradually as they are downloaded form the web. GIFs can also have multiple frames making simple animations possible. You can also choose a color that will be made transparent, allowing you to overlay images onto patterns.

an image saved as GIF at 256 colors

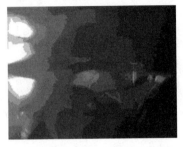

an image saved as GIF at 16 colors

JPEG

The JPEG breaks the image into squares, measuring eight by eight pixels, and describes each square mathematically. This is more effective for smooth areas of color than detailed edges, as it merges pixels into patterns of color. This is great for photographic imagery or graduations of color because their very nature hides this block pattern. It is possible for the JPEG to reduce a 24bit (millions of colors) photo into the same space as a GIF will save an 8-bit image, or less. However if you save images that have elements with sharp edges, this pattern shows up horribly and you can see the artifacts that it leaves.

The original letter saved as a gif

See how the jpeg smoothes and merges the pixels of the image, leaving marks around the edge where there were none before.

Optimizing Page Images for the Web

This is my page design. I have a high color photo in the background to save as a JPEG. The small colored panels are simple GIFs, but the text on these will be re-created using HTML, so I can hide that layer. The block on the far left has vertical text that HTML can't handle, so this will be saved on the GIF element underneath it. The large text will be saved as a GIF because it is in a special font; I can set its background as transparent to let the photo show through underneath.

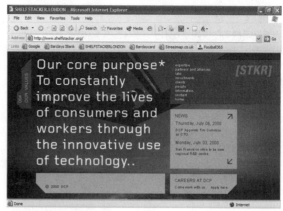

The text, colored blocks, and the background image will be arranged using layers in the HTML code, so I don't need to worry about splitting up my images for a table construction.

To Save Images for the Web

Before you use the web output tool, crop the image to the size you want:

1. Select the Crop tool from the toolbar.

2. Click in the top left hand corner of the area you wish to keep, drag, and release at the bottom right.

3. The 'doomed' area of your image appears darkened. You can adjust the edges of your selected area by dragging the little squares.

4. Finally, click on the tick on the Tool Options bar to accept the changes.

Once you're happy with the size, it's time to move on to saving and compressing the image.

1. Go to **File > Save for Web** to open the options dialog.

2. To the right of the screen are the options you have to work with. To the bottom of each image are its size, download time, and details.

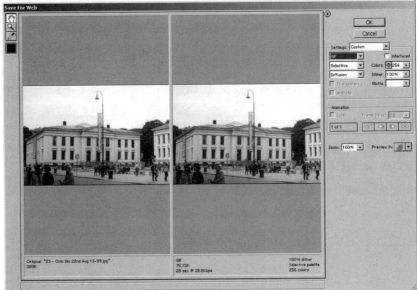

3. Check the zoom is set to 100% - this is the best reflection of the output in the final web browser.

As this is a photo, JPEG will probably be our best bet. If it were graphical, we'd probably choose either PNG or GIF.

4. To start with, we select JPEG Low Quality from the settings option box.

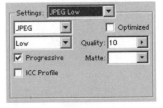

This reduces the JPEG quality to 10%, and the file size to 12.29K, but produces an unacceptable loss of quality. Look at the detailing around the lamp, and the color degradation around the edges of objects.

5. Dragging the quality slider up further reduces the artifacts, but at a more visually pleasing 30% quality, the image is now 19.16k, or 8 seconds at 28.8kbps

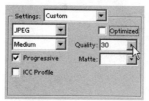

The trick to doing this is to keep an eye on the preview pane. You can start to see the patterns the JPEG compression makes at about 55% quality and below, but is your call as to how acceptable they will be to your audience.

TIP: It is general practice to keep reducing the file size until you can start to see a noticeable difference in quality. That is, unless you have a huge image and file size is going to have to be prioritized over quality.

6. Check the 'Progressive' box, as this means that when a browser loads the image, it can display information as it arrives, reducing the feeling of waiting for the user.

7. If you are happy with the result, click OK, which will bring up the traditional save dialog box.

TIP: It is good practice to save your images with a name that easily identifies it. As your site grows it will make things far more manageable.

Saving a Graphical or Animated File

If we are saving a more graphical file, then we are better off using GIFs or PNGs. If you want to animate the file, the computer will use each layer as one frame, so you may need to duplicate and flatten some layers.

1. Open the graphical file you wish to save for the web.

To save using this format, you don't need to have two layers, but if you do, you can animate them.

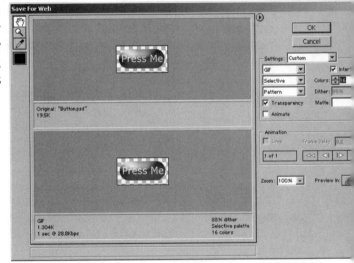

2. Click **File > Save For Web**... as before

3. This time select GIF in the box below the word settings, and then select a lower number in the Colors box to the right. Now it is time to make the compromise again, but 16 colors seemed reasonable for this graphic (which uses a lot of shades).

4. Now select the animate button. This will make the first layer (from the bottom) of your image layer 1, the second layer 2 and so on.

5. For this button, we only have two frames to flash from one to the other slowly. To do this we:

    ● Select 'Loop' so that the animation repeats itself.

    ● Change the frame delay to 2.0, so that the button changes state every two seconds.

Using this technique, and with a bit of time and thought, you can create far more complicated animations like those used in banner advertisements on the web.

Creating a Web photo gallery

In Photoshop Elements it is easy to publish a gallery of photos for use online. In fact all you have to do is tell Photoshop which folder of photos you want to use and it will automatically duplicate and resize the images, and create all the HTML that will be needed to view it on the Web and store all the elements in nice tidy folders.

You can then copy this into any web space that your service provider has given you and share your photos instantly. There are four different galleries and each one can be customized to your own style.

Simple displays thumbnails of all the images on a full page. Click on the image to see it full size, and use the arrows to cycle through all the images. This is fine for a small picture collection, but it would take a while to hunt for an image you like in a large gallery. You can also choose to have this first page of images displayed in a table.

Horizontal Frame splits the page into 2 areas, one for thumbnails of all the images that display in the second area when clicked. This is ideal for large albums. You can scan the images and click to view them without flipping backwards and forwards between pages. This type is also available in a vertical frameset, where the thumbnails are listed down the left-hand side.

Vertical Frame is the same, but its thumbnails are down the side of the page instead of along the bottom.

Table creates an HTML table

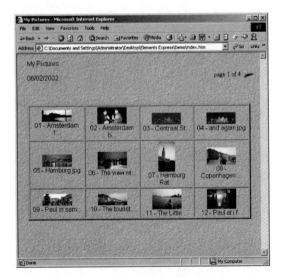

Creating a photo gallery

1. Ensure that all the pictures you want to use are stored in one folder on your computer, and you have made any changes or improvements that you want to.

2. Open the Web Photo Gallery options in **File > Automate > Web Photo Gallery.**

3. Select the final style that you want (here, we've selected Simple).

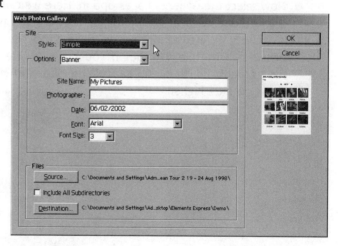

4. Select Banner on the Options pull-down menu (this option switches between various options in the rectangle below it). We'll look at all four of these option sets.

● Using the Banner option set, add a personal caption to the web pages we're creating in the top three boxes, and select the font and size in the bottom two.

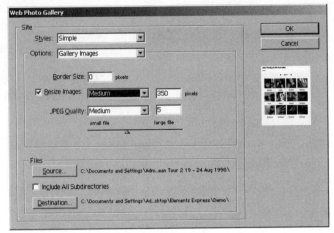

TIP: *When changing the font, remember that most people only have common fonts like Ariel on their computer*

● Now select the Gallery Images option. Here we can set the size and quality of the main images, set here at a width of 350 pixels. It's a good idea not to make it too much bigger because of the file size, but if you know all the viewers have broadband, then you can set the size, and even the quality, a little higher.

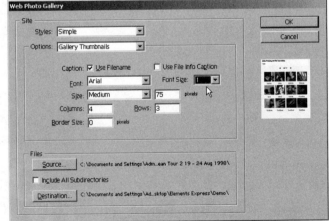

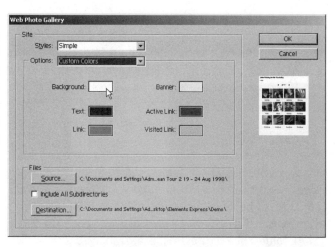

● The Gallery Thumbnails option allows you to set the size of thumbnails. It's a good idea to set the font size quite small, in order to get as much of the name on screen as possible. The Columns and Rows options have no effect on the Horizontal and Vertical frame styles.

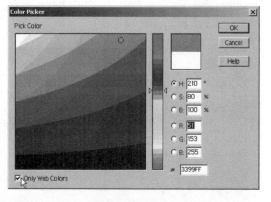

● The Custom Colors option allows you to define a different appearance for your pages. Clicking on a color brings up the color picker, from which we can select a color. It's a good idea to check the 'Web Safe Colors' in the bottom left corner, as this will ensure we select a color that can be reliably reproduced on other computers.

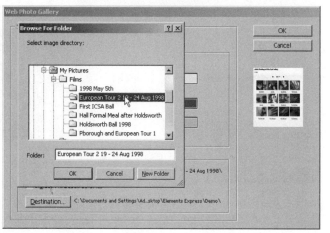

5. Once you're happy with the colors, all that remains is to set the folder that you want to create the web page from (the one with all the images in) and the output folder. Click on the Source button (near the bottom left) and use the pop-up window to select the folder where you keep your images. The computer will use these but leave them untouched.

6. Repeat this process with an output folder (it's best to save this in a new empty folder somewhere on your computer before uploading files to the Internet). This is where all the new files that form the web pages will be placed.

7. Click Finish

Once you've created the folder, you can upload it to the Internet using the instructions provided by your Internet service provider. It might also be a good idea to check the total file size first, as you often only get a few megabytes of web space (in this example a 18Mb folder of pictures made a 1Mb web site – tweaking the quality and size settings would have reduced the final size further).

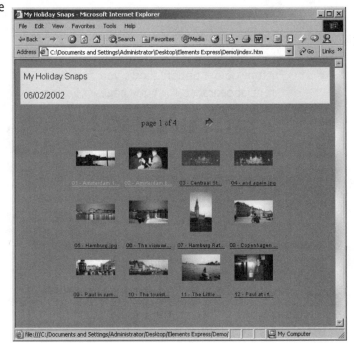

What's Next?

In the next section, we'll take a step-by-step look at creating a professional-looking image by using the tools and techniques we've looked at in the rest of the book. We will see how we can use layers, colors, selections, image manipulation, and more, to produce interesting and visually pleasing results.

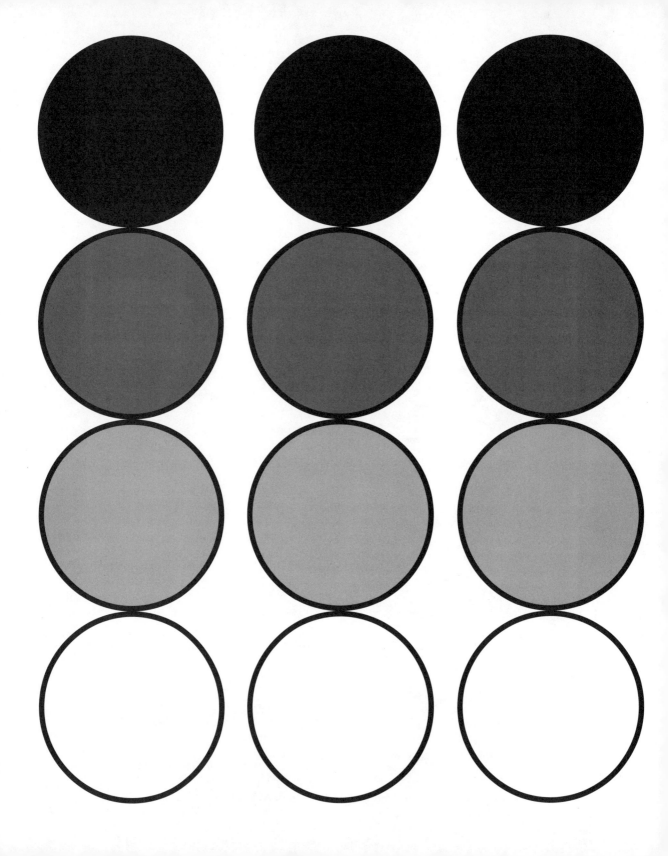

INSPIRATION 1

New Master: Gavin Cromhout

Occupation: Artist/designer

How did you get into design?

My grandfather was a landscape photographer, and he introduced me to the magic of seeing an image form out of nothing on a blank sheet of paper. I think that I became the designer I am as a result of carrying his heavy camera bag around for him. At first, photography had seemed like truth to me – a mirror held up to reality. But in the darkroom, I realized that photography could also be art.

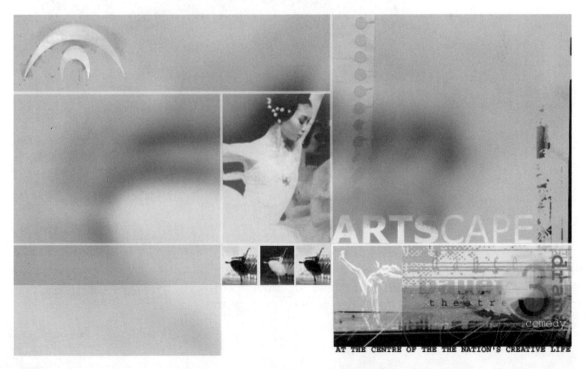

Why Photoshop?

Photoshop is not just its drawing tools, its editing tools, or its selection tools. The strength of Photoshop lies in the combination of all three, and you can only discover it through playing. Often, even if I think I already know which layer tool to use, I'll go through all the options, just to see. And most likely, I'll discover an effect that I can either use right there and then, or remember for later.

Talk about this design...

A lot of people try to go it alone, but I think it's important to look at other people's design. It's not a matter of copying, because no two designs are ever alike, but it's important to see why things work, and to remind yourself constantly of this.

You must build your final composition out of real, relevant, and complementary information – if you're creating a web site for an opera house, for example, use pictures of that opera house, not just stock images. If you include elements that are cohesive, the finished product carries another level of information that might not be immediately apparent, but which contributes towards a richer overall design.

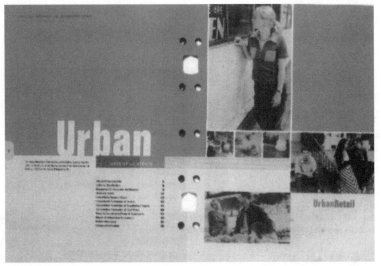

The first images I looked at were ones that dealt with breaking up the visual plain (like the page from a clothing catalogue shown here); this was something I wanted to get into my head before applying design styling. I applied my chosen colours (those given to me by my client; an olive-khaki-blue-green, ochre yellow and violet) to that basic design.

Having a go

The remainder of this chapter is a breakdown of how this image was created. It starts slowly, but as the techniques are re-used, it speeds up. If you get into difficulty, remember that all the techniques used in the creation of this artwork can be found in the rest of the book.

First Draft

I chose this picture of dancers for its striking presence. My initial plan was simply to leave the principal dancer in focus and blur everything else, but when I tried this technique it looked artificial. It's often that way with design: the way you picture something is very different from the way it comes out. Faced with this obstacle, I chose to differentiate the focused and blurred areas by segmenting the image.

Keeping one part of an image in focus and blurring the rest is particularly easy to achieve in Photoshop. All things considered, though, that's not a particularly aesthetic effect. I decided to break up my 'in focus' block a little further:

1. Open the file 1.dancers.psd.

2. Select a rectangle around the dancer and then inverse the selected area by pressing Ctrl/⌘-Shift-I or clicking Select > Inverse.

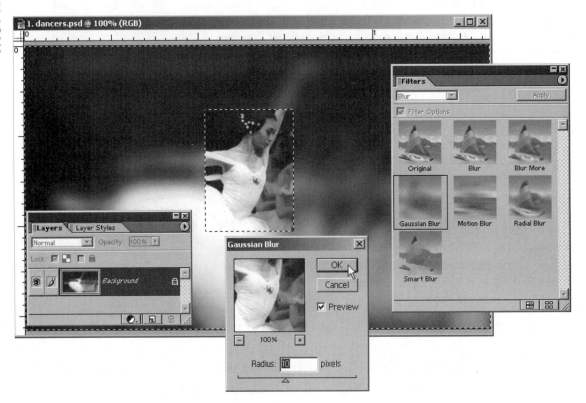

3. Click on the Background layer and apply a Gaussian blur with a radius of 12 pixels.

4. Press Ctrl/⌘-D to deselect the area afterward.

> TIP: If you upgrade to Photoshop 6 then you can create layer masks allowing you to move the blurred area after you have created it.

So. I've got my 'in focus' rectangle, as dictated by my layer mask. I found this contrast too stark, however. The next step is to adjust the hue and saturation for this part of the image.

1. Open the Hue/Saturation dialogue box by clicking Enhance > Color > Hue/Saturation, or by pressing Ctrl/⌘-U.

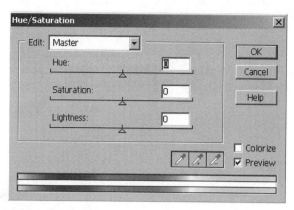

2. Adjust the sliders so that there is a hue value of 45 and a saturation value of 25.

At this stage, my plan to contrast the focused and blurred areas hadn't quite been carried off the way I wanted it, so I decided to add a new layer.

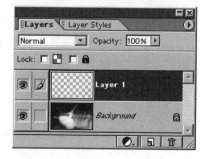

3. Create a new layer above the dancer background.

4. Click on the foreground color at the bottom of the toolbar and set it to a khaki color – I typed directly into the RGB boxes 231, 215, 163.

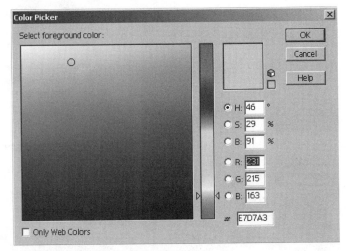

5. Using the Fill tool, apply this to the new layer. The dancer will completely disappear, but don't worry – she's still there.

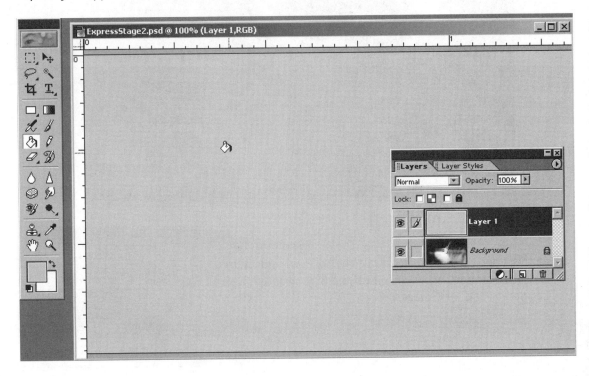

6. Adjust the opacity of the layer to 90% so that the dancer becomes slightly visible.

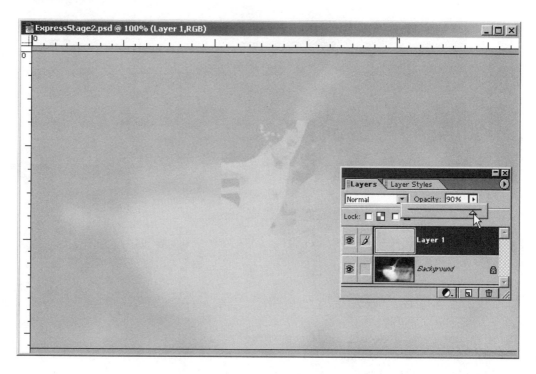

7. Now select the Eraser tool and set it to a largeish brush – say 100 pixels across – and a medium opacity using the tool options bar. Now gently begin to erase the colored layer around the detail of the dancer, thereby increasing the contrast over that area.

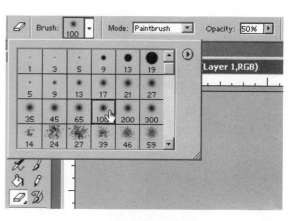

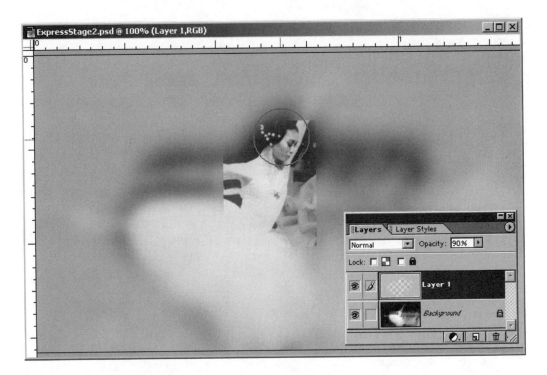

8. It should look a little like this. Once you've picked out the main area, reduce the opacity (to, say, 10%) and go around the edges to soften them.

> TIP: You can also use the smudge tool here if you prefer it.

9. Once you are happy with the way you've picked out your dancer, reset the opacity of the layer to 100%. You might also want to give the layer a sensible name – I've chosen Khaki Mask.

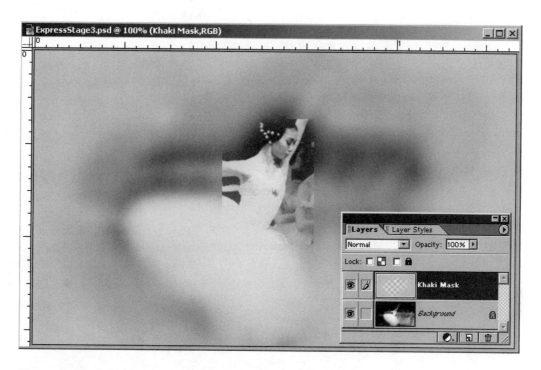

The effect of all of this is to contrast the in-focus and blurred areas, but in a less obvious and more interesting way. Also, the refinement of the contrast between the in-focus dancer and the blurred background has increased the surface depth of the work. It's not just totally flat, and that added volume draws the viewer in.

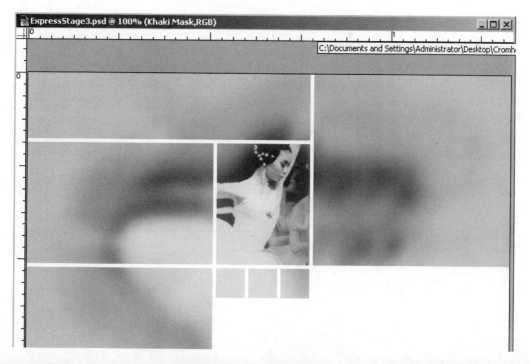

Now it's time to apply the structural shapes, culled from the clothing catalogue. Perhaps the easiest way to do this is by using the grid feature.

1. Switch on the grid using View > Show Grid.

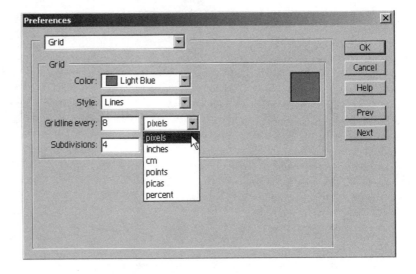

2. If you don't think that the lines are narrow enough, you can adjust them using the preferences menu. Simply click Edit > Preferences > Grid....

3. Set View > Snap (unless it is already checked).

4. Select the Line tool and set the width to 3pt using the Tool Options bar.

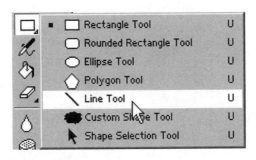

5. Ensure the foreground color is set to white, and draw the grid pattern. Holding down Shift will ensure that the lines stay at the correct angle rather than exactly following the cursor.

6. Once the grid looks like this, you can turn off the grid and snap features. The next step is to merge the layers:

- Click the link buttons in each shape layer.

- Merge the layers you just linked by clicking on the palette menu button and selecting Merge Linked.

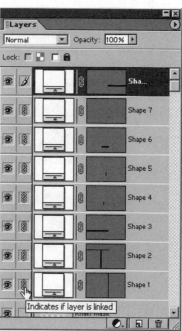

195

7. Finally, create a new layer for the white areas, draw rectangles (using the Rectangle tool, tucked behind the Line tool) and then pop the whole layer behind our grid.

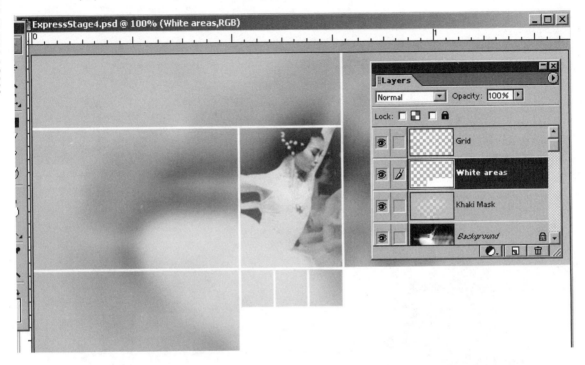

Once the guides are sorted out, it's time to drop in the smaller image and start working on the rest of the collage.

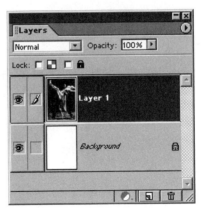

1. Open the file `smalldancers.psd` and drag the dancers layer into the picture we're working on.

2. The image is a little too large for us, not to mention appearing in the wrong spot. Once it appears, click Image > Transform > Free Transform (or pres Ctrl/⌘-T).

3. Using the tool options bar, click on the link button (between the W and H boxes) and then change one to read 80%. Both should update automatically.

4. Now drag the image into position.

5. With that done, use the Rectangular Marquee tool to select the dancers and the area to the right of them.

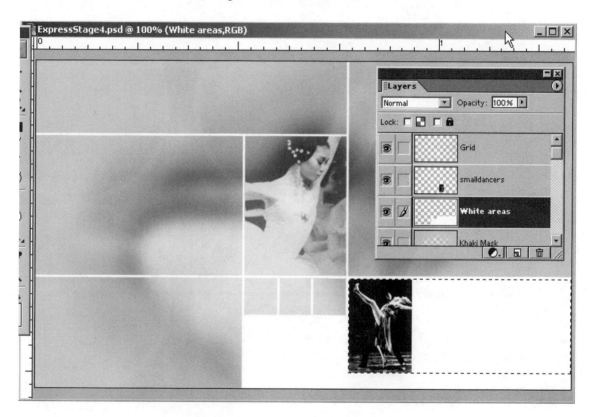

6. Ensure that the white areas layer is selected, and not the small dancers layer, then press the delete key.

7. Now, with the selection still active, click Layer > New Adjustment Layer > Hue/Saturation…. In the resulting dialogue turn the saturation right down and click OK.

TIP: If you lose your selection, press Ctrl-Shift-D or Select > Reselect to bring back the last selection boundary.

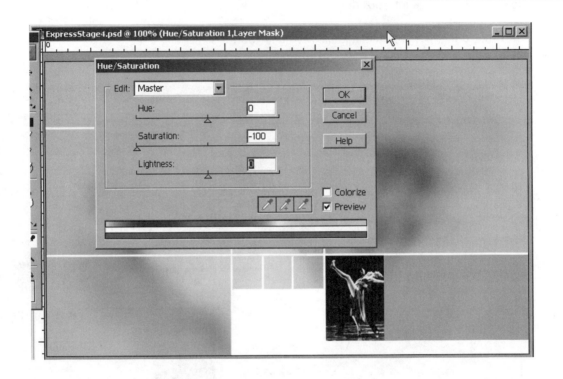

8. With the selection still active, create a new layer and fill it completely in a rich yellow (I used RGB: 255, 204, 0). Drag this above the dancers in the Layers palette and set the blending mode to Screen.

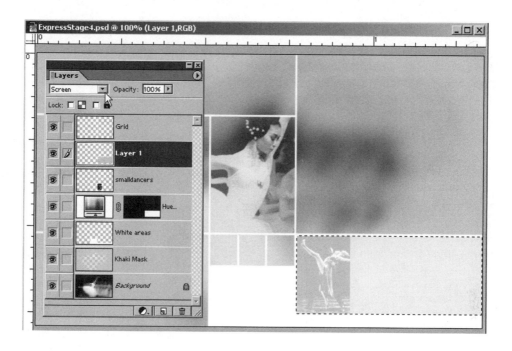

9. Deselect the area we've been working on using Ctrl-D.

Although the top-right section of the image is broken up to some degree by the blurred remains of the dancers, I wanted to increase this. I scanned in the messed up sides of an old photocopy – a perfect place to find some really interesting shapes and textures!

1. Open the image file (scanned_in.psd).

2. Drag the breakup layer into the main image

3. Use the Move tool (see right) to rotate the  image. Holding down the shift key, move the pointer near the edge of image and rotate the image 90° counter-clockwise before releasing the mouse button then the shift key.

4. Click somewhere in the middle and drag the photocopy edge to the side of our artwork.

5. Now scale it to fit the side, holding shift as you drag the corner node to maintain the proportions.

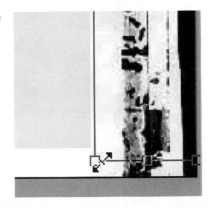

6. Once you're happy with the size, move the layer behind the yellow rectangle we created earlier.

7. Set the layer blending mode to 'Multiply'.

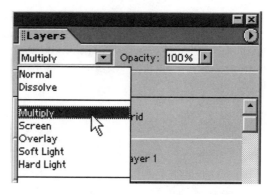

8. With the layer still selected, use the Eraser tool to soften the edges.

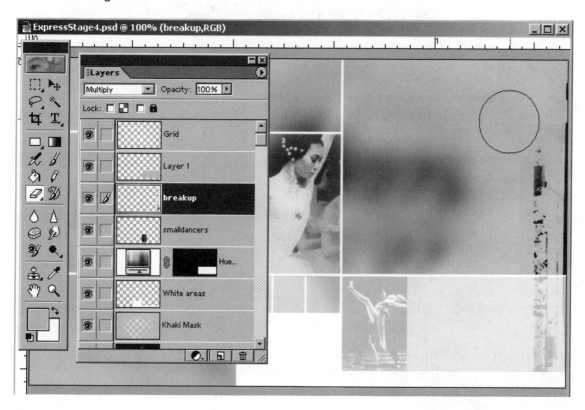

TIP: *As you complete layers you can check the lock box at the top of the layer to ensure you don't affect it as you continue to work.*

The yellow panel of the collage is a complex piece to look at in the final form, but there are distinct elements, and it was constructed in a particular order that we will now look at. I wanted to try representing every aspect of theatre using text in an abstract technique.

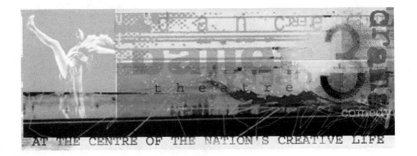

Rather than get lost in the detail of how each of these text layers is added, we'll just look at them in the order they were added. To follow the example, choose your own fonts, as everyone seems to have a different set on their computer.

1. The dance layer is written below our yellow screen, using spaces to separate the characters (it's quick and easy). The text is written in black.

2. The word ballet is also added beneath the screen, but it is then converted from text to graphics (right/ctrl-click the layer in the palette and select Simplify Layer), and then the top of the characters is deleted.

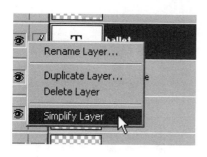
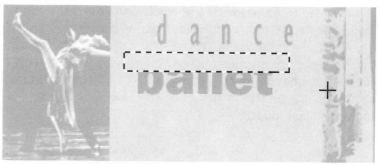

3. The word 'opera' is inserted, turned upside-down and moved above the yellow screen layer in the layers palette. It is set to overlay. In order to make it a stronger effect, an identical copy layer is placed above using the Duplicate Layer... option.

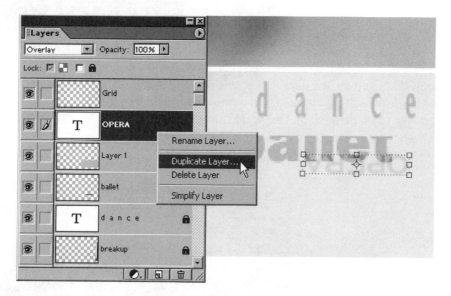

4. The theatre text layer, and the byline 'The nation's creative life' are above the others written in standard black. They are moved into position using the cursor keys to 'nudge' them into position.

I now wanted to add elements that would cause the text to break up further. To the text, I added four bits of texture, the first of which was a scanned-in corner of an old photograph (`morebreakup.psd`), all scratched up (ready to serve!), which I added to the bottom of the rectangular area. I named the layer photobreakup, inverted it (Image > Adjustments > Invert), and applied Multiply mode.

On top of this, I added a textured block of yellow color (`breakup.psd`), on a new layer called yellowover, also with a blending mode of Multiply. I wanted to saturate the lower half of the rectangle with color, partly so that the word comedy (which I'd done in white) was more visible, and partly so that the photobreakup layer could be toned down (I felt it was a little too dominant).

The third bit of texture is a few blown up lines from a fax form. (You'll be amazed where you can find texture!) I added this above the photograph texture on a new layer called photocopy. Again, I used Multiply mode here.

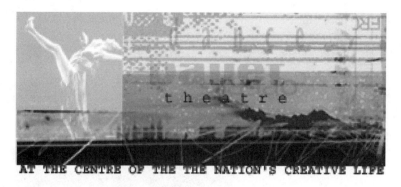

The fourth piece of texture was a scratchy photograph of an old film number countdown sequence (film3.psd). I used the eraser tool to get rid of the edges of the photograph. I must admit that this last insertion was a little off the theme, and I did think about that at the time. However, I was going for the 'art across all mediums' approach, so I took a little artistic license myself!

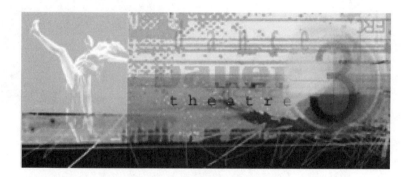

You'll have noticed that I used Multiply mode on a lot of the layers. The reason for this is that using Multiply allows for intersections between layers to be visible – you can see through the top layer to the layer underneath. Also, unlike Overlay or Screen, you don't lose a lot of the substance of the layer. Another reason why I used this particular blending mode was that I didn't want the upper layers to dominate those underneath them. Putting everything on one layer would solve this, of course, but then I would have lost the flexibility to change things later.

At this point, I added two further bits of text – drama and comedy over the '3' – though the word drama is set to colour burn and 88% opacity and tucked below the 'photobreakup' layer.

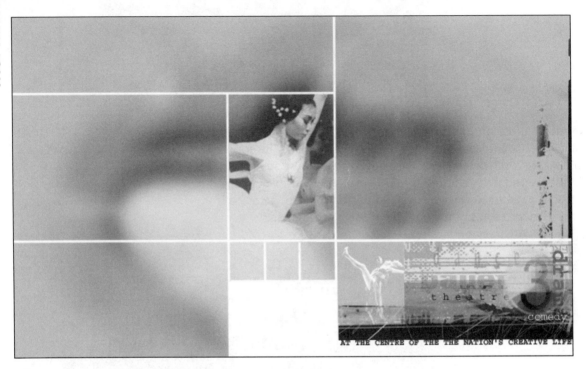

The result, I think, has a very gritty look and feel. The reason I went for this is that the theater is currently in a process of transformation, of reinventing itself. Part of this process is the deconstruction of the idea that theater is inaccessible to youth – they don't want to be seen as a staid, boring old place. I've tried to bring across a feel of street culture, with an 'alleyway torn-down poster' combined with a 'digital information-flow'. Certainly it's a strange mix of ideas, but I was anxious to move the design into a funkier highland.

At this point I added the Artscape logo I had been supplied, and softened it a little using the eraser tool again.

At this point, I sent the work off to the client for comments. While they liked the progress, they were concerned with the way the 'Artscape' text was so badly broken up. I guess I was messing with their corporate identity too much, so I went back and toned down the grid layer.

Final Draft

The final step is to make the design more web-like, so it can form the basis of a web page, so some elements for navigation would be required. Second, the one negative comment that I received from the client was that the design was very ballet-centric. There was a reason, though: I planned for the site to be extremely customizable, to the extent that a viewer would be able to choose a different skin/theme when they came to the site. This, therefore, was the ballet theme. While a lot of the elements would stay the same across themes (it's always a bad idea to change how navigation works, for example), I planned to replace the dancers with (say) opera singers – a similar look, but a different feel. This idea was well met with by the client.

Unfortunately I had to abandon one of my earliest ideas – to have a sequence of the dancer in slightly changing poses, like a filmstrip – as I just couldn't get hold of any satisfactory raw material. I still liked the idea though, so I decided to use the same image, repeated in different tones.

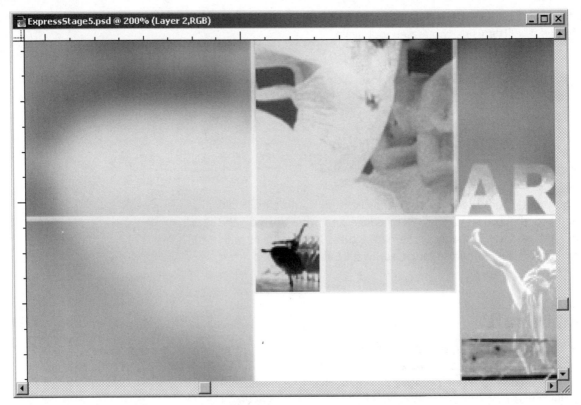

ExpressStage5.psd @ 200% (Layer 2,RGB)

I created the three distinct images by inserting one thumbnail of the original ballerina and adjusting the hue/saturation and the layer blending style for each one. This is a great opportunity to play around and see what you like (I used normal, exclusion and luminosity).

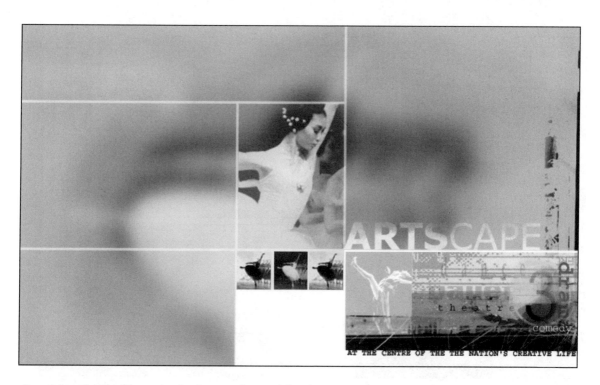

One thing that had been bothering me for a while, though, was the inequality of different sections of the work: some sections were sticking together, and others weren't. This was spreading the focus of the work too much, which is something I wanted to remedy by segmenting it further. I therefore selected the bottom left section, and applied an adjustment layer to lighten it up.

I did this, as before, by selecting the area I wanted to adjust, clicking Layer > New Adjustment Layer > Hue/Saturation....

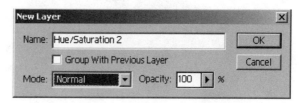

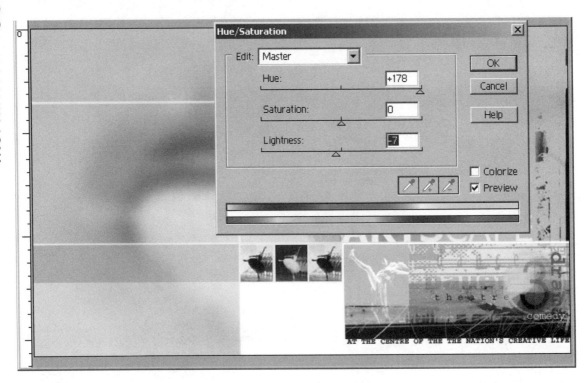

The flow of the work was still bothering me, so I added some new design in the largest panel. For this, I used a scanned-in piece of torn, ring-bound paper (ringunbound.psd) with a Luminosity blending mode at around 30% opacity.

I then used the eraser to soften the end (as I did before) then I used the Magic Wand tool to select and delete the remaining dark areas of the image.

With this completed, all that remained was to crop off the bottom of the image, something I only ever do right at the end of a project – just in case I need to use the space, and wind up constricting myself. Finally, I added the Artscape logo in the top left, and broke it up (just a little) to match the Artscape text.

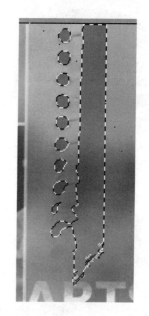

Conclusion: Revisiting the Theme

With the constant reworking of the horizontal and vertical flow, and the break-up of the images, I feel that I've created a fairly strong focal point to the work, centered roughly on the beginning of the "Artscape" text. Also, there's a prevalent diagonal flow to the work (from top left to bottom right), which works from an information point of view: first the logo, then the company name, then the by-line, but picking up visual information the whole way through this journey. This is certainly something I tried to create throughout the design process: a strong sense of visual flow.

On viewing the (now completed) image, I feel that my constant reworking has, to some extent, lost the initial impact of having one dancer in focus, and the rest blurred. This was prevalent in the early versions of the work, but got 'designed over' as things progressed. It's not entirely lost, but if I could change anything, it would be to reintroduce this feature somehow. A positive outcome, on the other hand, is that the reworking has given the design a good surface depth. There are many different levels to the design, some clearly in focus, and some unformed.

I've gone from the idea of representing the concepts of art and literature fairly literally, to a more 'street hype' kind of style. I think the balance of the work might have tipped a little too far towards the funky end, but I feel this travel of concept is a good one. Anyway, old people can be cool too...

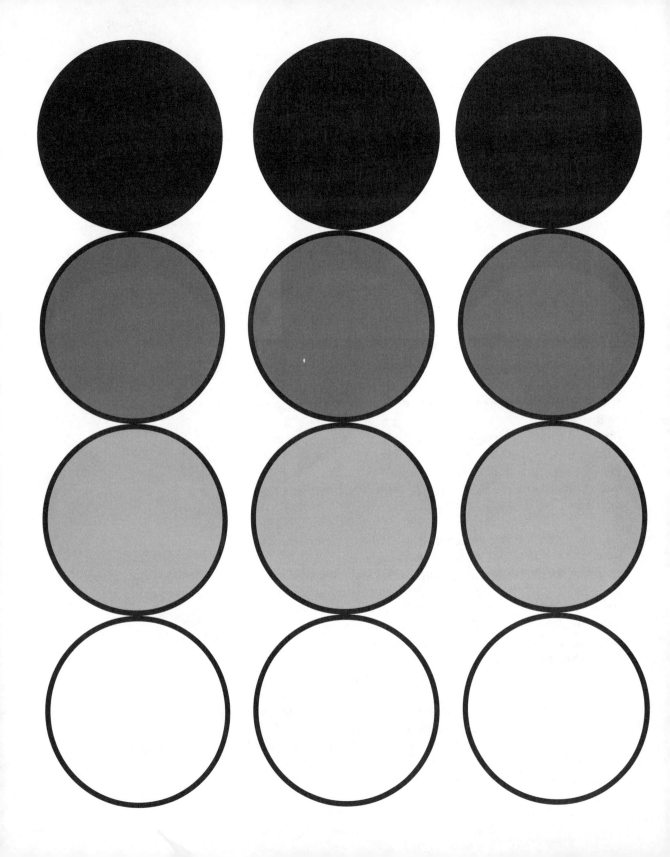

INSPIRATION 2

Designer: Jim Hannah

Why Photoshop?

As well as being the first requirement on any designer's resume, Photoshop is probably the ultimate geek's tool. I mean, look at it. It's very powerful and it allows you to do just what you want to whatever pictures you like.

The trouble is, computers are sniffed at by a lot of artists. Of course, you've got to understand it. When I see a Disney movie with a computer-animated sequence in it, I feel a stir of disappointment that some poor sap didn't sweat over each frame of film, hand-animating one second every three months.

But let's get some perspective here. Remember what it was like to discover that you could now digitize all your old family pictures from the Sixties or Fifties or Forties? All of a sudden they're fixed forever as good quality prints – just like new!

Then you have to question what you are going to do with these amazing new picture files. Print them out! Print them out again! And again!

It's dumb, really, isn't it? But there is something inherently fulfilling about that, and I refuse to ignore that initial rush of goodwill. Photoshop makes me feel better, quickly.

Talk about this design...

I've always had to try and push my design skills towards something more figurative, and I think that's a good idea when you're trying to start something in Photoshop. I admire a lot of the abstract compositions, but it's very easy to fall into the trap of just putting a picture together for no reason – then of course you're stuck as to how to show it to people – or why.

So, I came up with this design which I wanted to put towards a greetings card for a friend of mine. The brief I came up with was to utilize Photoshop to produce an image which has a certain amount of animation to it. It's got to be intuitive and interesting – and this is what Photoshop is good at.

The Sky

The first thing I wanted to do was get a good looking sky together. If you live where I do, you'll find that serviceable skies are few and far between, so you have to be prepared. I took the opportunity of snapping a lovely winter sky a while back. The complete picture is made up of three shots of an enormous and threatening cloud, so all I had to do was scan the images in – that's right, I can't afford a decent digital camera.

Of course, you have the image files ready-digitized, but for the record I did this by hitting File > Import and selecting my scanner from the drop-down menu. Up popped my scanner interface, and I scanned each image in.

Being the impatient type, I was simultaneously sending emails and running a CD-ROM. The end result of this was that my scanner stopped halfway through and refused to go any further. This, then, is your handy hint: Close everything down while you're scanning. It's just better for all concerned. Between you and me, if you still have problems, you might look to use your scanner's simple image-acquiring software just to complete this task. Chances are it's not going to hog your computer's resources in the way Photoshop does – and it'll do the job just as well.

I saved each of the pictures as PSD files, named `sky1`, `sky2` and `sky3`.

1. So, to fix them together, we'll us the handy (if entertainingly erratic) Photomerge tool. Click on File > Photomerge. Click on the Add button and browse to the location of the `sky1`, `sky2` and `sky3` files.

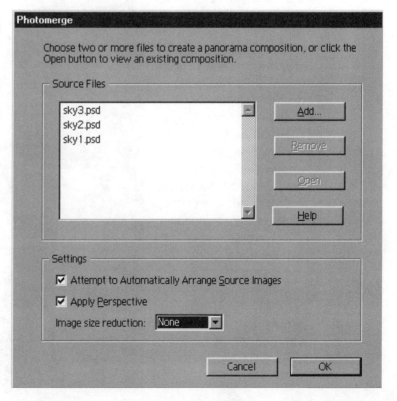

2. The images will slowly be loaded onto a single canvas. You will be able (after the Automatic Arrangement tool has got it completely wrong) to move things around a bit, and you should aim to end up with something like the following:

...two thirds of which I think makes for a pretty good panorama. But that vertical line between the first two photographs, well, that's no good.

3. This calls for some swift Photoshop techniques. Not all of them are very subtle, but all of them are effective. The best thing to do in a situation like this is to divide the various sections up into simpler tasks – don't try to fix the whole thing in one fell swoop. First we have the sky. This is the easiest bit, because skies are very forgiving of retouching. Select a biggish area with the Polygonal Lasso tool and applied a strong motion blur (Filter > Blur > Motion Blur). This wrecks the dividing line between the photographs – so there we have one smooth sky.

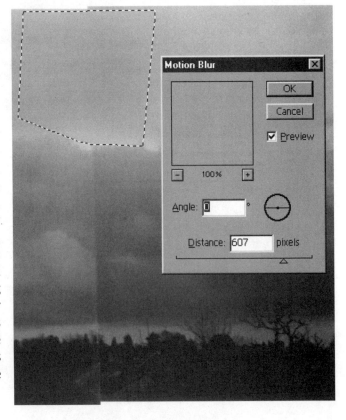

4. Next comes the more tricky bit – those bubbly clouds. The image difference is very noticeable here, so it calls for a bit more creativity. The best tool I've found for fixing this is the Clone Stamp tool. This tool is really a great piece of work, but it can be very badly applied if you're not careful. In order to whittle away the line in the clouds, set the tool's opacity to 45%, and used a soft round 100-pixel brush from the brush dropdown menu.

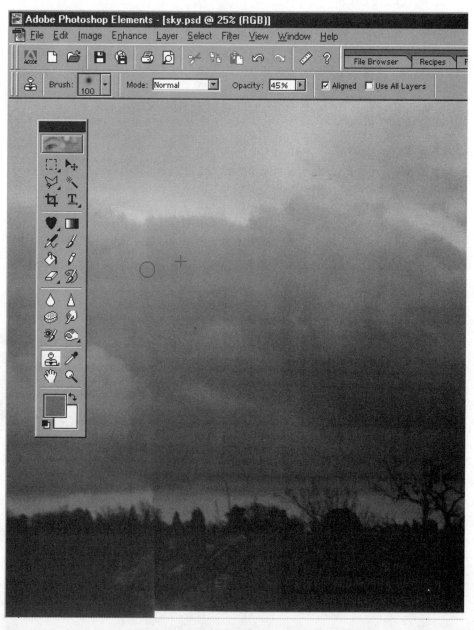

Just pushing a little of the dark into the light side, and a little of the light into the dark will soon have that line muffled. This really is a case when your artistic efforts will make or break the cover-up – it's just like painting with oils. The same technique should neutralize the bit of sky just above the horizon.

5. As for the last bit – the dark landscape – well, there's no need to fuss about that too much. It's not important in the grand scheme of things, so pick a hard-edged brush and use the Clone Stamp tool once again to average it all out. Several residents may have their houses obliterated, but it's all in the name of art.

6. For your own piece of mind, you may like to perform a few similar techniques on the other join, between pictures 2 and 3, just to polish up what the Automatic Arrangement tool may have missed. Then, using the Crop tool, cut off those jagged white edges, and you'll end up with something like this:

The perfect widescreen skyline. Save it as `skyFINAL.psd` and stow it somewhere safe.

The Foreground

When you're looking to put photographs together, there are times when Automatic just won't do. If you look back to the completed image, you will see that the figure's arms overlap in several places. This means that the photographs must overlap. And you can bet your bottom dollar that the Automatic Arrangement tool isn't going to ask us how we want that to happen. It doesn't care whether we want any single element in front of any other.

So, another technique is required. My favored system is the judicious use of Layers.

So to set the scene – we have seven photographs, which constitute a foreground. I went out and took them especially to go with the sky I'd already put together. They combine to create a panorama, but with the added touch of a figure placed in the middle. In this way I created a stop-frame effect of a figure walking across a landscape.

1. Open the first one, `walk1.psd`. The first thing to do is to make space beside it in order to drop in the second image. So, go through Image > Resize > Canvas Size. Within that dialog box I made the settings below, which expanded the canvas to 200% of its original size.

Because we are anchoring the existing photograph to the middle-left of the canvas, Photoshop bundles the extra space to the right. Onto this new canvas you will be able to drop the second picture. You should also add a little height, as the next picture was likely to need placing a little way below the current one.

2. So, open the second image file, walk2.psd. There are thousands of ways to get that image down onto my main

canvas, but the simplest is the best. With both pictures visible, use the Move tool to drag the second picture onto the first.

3. The good thing about this is that Photoshop automatically puts this image on a new layer, so we don't have to worry about creating it ourselves. Now, move the second image around to roughly line it up with the first.

The important thing with this image is to get the background to appear solid. It doesn't matter what the figure's doing, so long as the background is smooth and believable. So the trees in the background are the best markers by which to line up the image. The tall fir in the background appears in both images, so why not use that?

4. Here we hit another snag: In trying to line those firs up, the second image simply rolls in front of the first, and you can't see the fir on the bottom image. We need some way of

seeing them both at the same time. The best way I found of working around this was by tweaking the Opacity of the top layer. Take a look at the Layers palette, and set the Opacity to 60%.

5. This allows us to line those firs up properly. However, you'll notice that although they themselves are more or less spot on, the curb towards the bottom of the picture is slightly out. Fix this by dragging the bottom-right anchor point of the see-through image inwards to make it slightly smaller. By keeping the Shift key pressed while doing this, you will make sure everything stays in proportion.

6. The next thing to deal with – as I stated before – is the overlap of the first figure's arm with the second image.

We can still see the first figure's hand and part of her coat through the translucent second image, so all we need to do is trace around that shape and – making sure you are still on the second layer – press delete. This removes the excess background and ensures that arm appears to overlap the join.

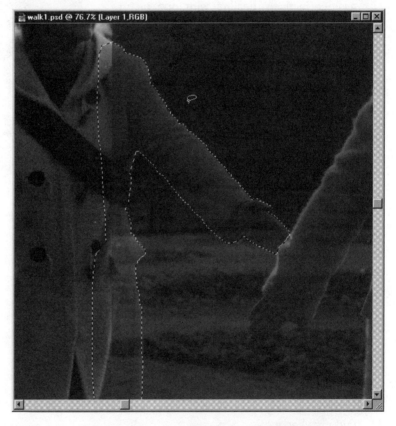

7. To be absolutely sure this join will look okay, before you press delete, try entering a value into the Feather box on the Lasso tool options.

A 2-pixel feather will make the delete a little softer at the edges, avoiding a really obvious edit, and helping that coat to stay fluffy!

8. Now it's safe to lift the second picture's Opacity back up to 100% and see what we have to contend with. The result is nothing too taxing. Just a bit of a line that can easily be obliterated with the Clone Stamp tool.

Before you set to this, flatten the two layers (Layer > Flatten Image) so you are once again effectively dealing with one picture. The colors blend better that way. One thing you should bear in mind at this point is the fact that the trees in the background are unlikely to make the final composition, so concentrate your efforts on the foreground.

Back to Square Three

Now it is time to start all over again with the third of the seven foreground images. Once again enlarging the Canvas width (by 200% again, for the time being), drop the new image in as before. Reduce the opacity, manoeuvre it this way and that, resize it a bit, and finally settle on its new position, with the background rock steady.

Once again, cut out the area of picture that gets in the way of the previous figure's arm, leaving the fluffy 2-pixels of feathering. Push the new image's Opacity back up to 100% and, hey presto! Ah, hold on a second.

Something is amiss between these photographs:

...and it's the weather. In the fraction of a second between the second and third figures you can clearly see the sun has come out. Of all the rotten luck! Nature's own Brightness/Contrast tool has provided a lovely sharp shadow where there wasn't one before. This is why not having a digital camera is so much fun. There's no going back and taking the photograph again. The changeable climate is now committed to celluloid.

Now, if you're thinking we should have a go at it with our own Brightness/Contrast tool, you'd be right. But, wisdom has to kick in first. It would be best to lay out the final four pictures, to see whether the sun remains out. We have to know whether we're going to make everything brighter or duller.

So, using exactly the same techniques as already outlined, that's what to do. Note: as we're looking to change the color dynamics of whole layers, don't merge the layers just yet.

So, there's the damage. When I put the full, unblended panorama together, I cursed the day I enthusiastically took my film off to be processed in a special 20 minute deal at the local developer's. I mean, personal mistakes I can put up with. Even atmospheric change has me shrugging and saying *c'est la vie*. But when shoddy developing produces the inconsistency of color apparent in picture 5, well, that really gets my goat.

There's nothing else for it, we'll have to see what Photoshop can do. As I had four bright images and three dark, I decided to try and make the whole thing bright. It's less work and I'm anxious to finish as soon as possible.

I decided to start with the rogue picture 5. Looking at it, the main sticking point is the concrete.

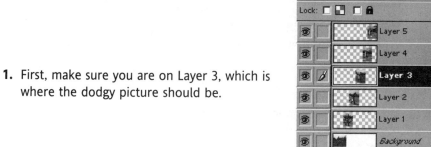

1. First, make sure you are on Layer 3, which is where the dodgy picture should be.

2. Then, with the Polygonal Lasso tool, select the gray ground in the picture. I'd advise you zoom in as much as possible to get this done – it saves a lot of best-guessing.

You will notice that the selections between the trouser legs and in front of the front foot are separate from the main selection. Such multiple selections can be achieved by pressing Shift and starting afresh with the Lasso.

3. The problem with the picture is, it's too dark, so instinct took me to the Fill Flash tool (Enhance > Fill Flash). Judging by the comparative lightness of the path beside it, nudge the Fill Flash value up until you have a reasonable match.

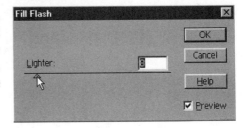

What is instantly noticeable is the fact that we seem to have a blue hue attacking our path. This can easily be sorted by adjusting the Hue/Saturation values.

4. It's simple really. Too much blue? Get rid of it. Go to Enhance > Color > Hue/Saturation – or press CTRL + U. From the Edit dropdown menu, select Blues. Never one to go by halves, I suggest you slide the slider hard left to a value of –100. This eliminates the blues altogether, but leaves untouched that lovely ginger-green lichen on the ground.

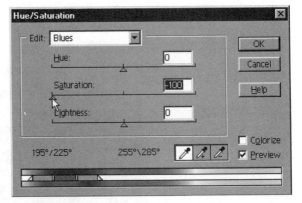

5. I also think we have too much red in there. What were they *doing* with those chemicals at the developers? Anyway, it's easily fixed: just select Reds from the Hue/Saturation palette and this time slip the Lightness slider up to 100.

6. A little extra tweak with the Brightness/Contrast (Enhance > Brightness/Contrast > Brightness/Contrast), and I think we've got something we can work with.

So, leave that for the time being and concentrate on the first two pictures, where Mother Nature played a little trick. These pictures, as you will remember, were the first two we dealt with. We merged them both onto the background layer – so make sure in the Layers palette you have Background selected.

The thing to look out for is the color balance between the shades of grass in these pictures. That is the most obvious change.

So, that's what to attend to first.

1. On the Magic Wand tool options, set the Tolerance to 40. Starting from the left, click on the grass, and it will become surrounded by a marquee. How did I know this was the right Tolerance level? By getting it wrong about five times before arriving at this figure. If the grass isn't all selected, hold down SHIFT and click on it – this should bring it into line. Notice that some of the marquee bleeds over the edge of our dark grass on to the light grass. Don't worry about this – it's selecting the picture *underneath* the light grass.

2. With all the grass selected, head back to the Fill Flash tool (Enhance > Fill Flash) and set it to about 20. That pretty much sorts the levels out, but again we have that slightly blue hue to things, so we're going to have to tweak that. It doesn't do to have luminous grass.

3. Go to Enhance > Color > Hue/Saturation and this time leave the Edit drop down on Master. We're going to be hard-nosed and force all those colors into line. Simply setting Hue to −30 gives the grass that exact yellowy-green tinge we're after.

4. Next, select the concrete path – that's still pretty glum. I suggest using your favorite marquee tool for this, as the Magic Wand is liable to get mixed up with the figure's trousers. Bring up the Hue/Saturation palette (Ctrl/⌘ U) and select the Blues to edit. Trial and error led me to select −23 as about the right Hue setting, with the Brightness rolled right up to +100. Without pressing OK, head back to the Master selection from the Edit dropdown and nudge the Brightness up to around +15. Again, this gets us to a state we can work with.

5. Okay, if everyone's happy, it's time to take the plunge. Layer > Flatten Image.

6. To get the picture looking smooth and realistic, work at those vertical lines using exactly the techniques used on the cloud picture back at the start. Again, don't worry too much about the sky and trees – they'll be gone soon enough.

After a little tampering, here's what I ended up with:

7. Where I was still having a few problems with color variation, I employed the Dodge and Burn tools to calm things down a bit. These tools can be a little bit over-enthusiastic, so I suggest picking a relatively small brush size for them, and adopting a low Exposure value in the Options palette. This will enable you to paint with light in much the same way photographers have for a century or more.

8. You will also notice I have cropped the image somewhat to hide all of those unseemly edges. At the bottom left of the composition, a couple of white rectangles remained, so I filled those in with concrete using the Clone Stamp tool. Simple, really! That's the beauty of this image – so long as you are sparing and judicious with the effects, everything is very simple.

9. There's really only one giveaway sign that this was more than one photograph – apart from the slim chances of identical septuplets – and that is the cropping of the shadows. There are two options here: draw them in, or get rid of them altogether. Now, this is a real stinker. If the complete shadows were all there, the image would look fantastic. But they're not – and if we draw them in, there's a very good chance they'll look extremely fake.

So, with a heavy heart, and using the two left-most figures as an example, I decided to get rid of them using the Clone Stamp tool. By way of consolation I opted to hint at shadows with the Burn tool.

Reaching for the Sky

OK, now it's time to bring everything together.

1. First, using Canvas Size, expand the canvas to make way for the sky. Remember to anchor the picture at the bottom of the screen.

2. Next, make a note of the exact width of the picture in pixels. You will find this in Image > Resize > Image Size.

3. Open up skyFINAL.psd. Go to Image > Resize > Image Size and type in the same width, making sure Constrain Proportions and Resample Image Bicubic are both checked. This will ensure the sky should fit snugly onto our foreground canvas. To find out, drag it over:

4. The simple final move will see us plant the top horizon on the bottom one, without performing head-removal surgery on each of the seven walking figures. The thing to do, as before, is to bring the sky layer down to an Opacity of, say, 50%. Then, bring it down to the horizon of the foreground image.

5. Now we can start our old trick of cutting away the excess background to reveal the figures:

Remember to Feather the selection to make the cut a little less severe.

6. When you are satisfied with these cuts, bring the horizon layer back up to 100% Opacity and admire your work! You can now flatten the image (Layer > Flatten Image) and make any minor amendments that your artistic sensibilities just won't let you ignore. Mine nagged on at me about the foliage at the right edge, and how it clashed with the black horizon. So, I Clone Stamped it into submission, noticing as I did a little man sitting on a bench in the distance. I hadn't seen him in real life!

Hopefully this little canter through the more photo-realistic aspects of Photoshop Elements has left you enthused about what to do with your own pictures. Don't forget – rooting your images in practicality can present all sorts of creative challenges. Now with a mastery of this software, you should be equal to them all.

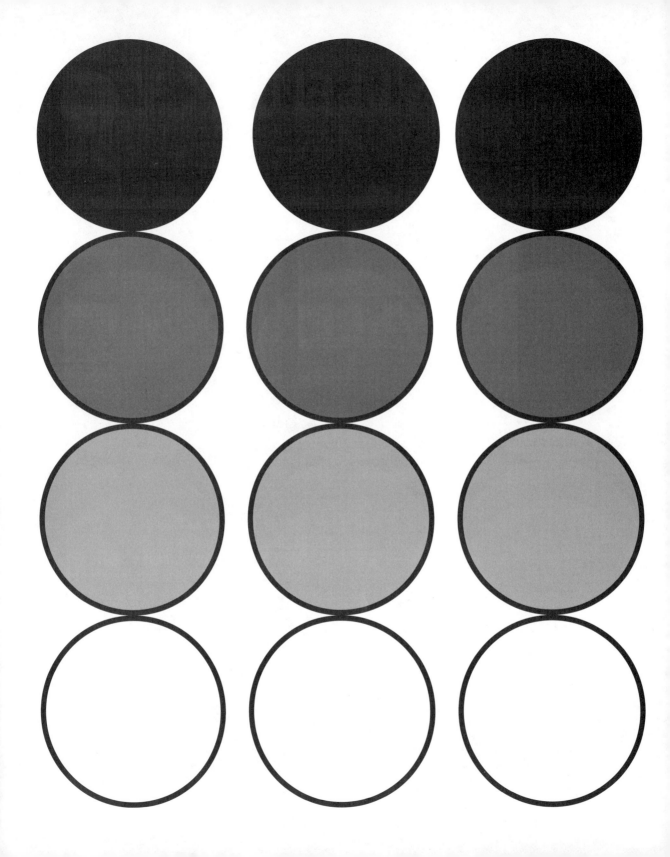

APPENDIX A

Photoshop Elements didn't come from nowhere, but is in fact a home version of the venerable Photoshop, first released in 1990 and still Adobe's flagship product. The most recent version at time of going to press was Photoshop 6. It is without a doubt the most successful package for bitmap image editing on both the PC and the Mac and an essential part of any designers toolkit.

What's the difference? Luckily for Elements users, the interface and many of the tools are basically the same, but there are one or two surprises for those swapping between the two. Here the basic differences are listed to help users familiar with one version make the transition to the other.

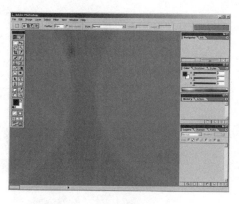 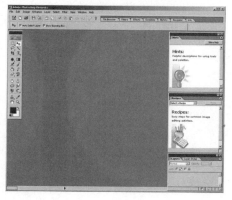

Look and Feel

Both programs work in a very similar way, with the Toolbox, Tool Options Bar and palettes approach to work. Photoshop 6, however, lacks the Shortcuts bar at the top of the screen, and by default all the palettes are nestled behind each other rather than stored in the Palette Well at the top of the screen.

Different Palettes

Photoshop 6 includes some different palettes, and does not include the File Browser, Recipe or Hints palettes.

Colors Palette

The Colors palette allows you to select colors without going through the color-picker, and it also works in Cyan/Magenta/Yellow/Key mode as well as RGB allowing you to specify exactly how much ink your printer uses. Professional color separation is also necessary to achieve effects like knock out which are simply not possible in Elements.

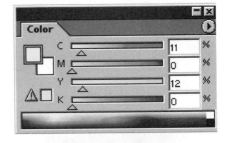

Channels Palette

Enhancing Photoshop's ability to work in CMYK, the Channels palette allows you to view and work with each separate color or ink (or in Red, Green and Blue) in much the same way as you can with layers. This makes it easier to achieve subtle color enhancements, as well as a variety of other effects.

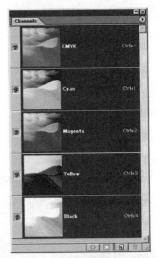

Actions Palette

Photoshop 6 allows you to record things you've done and repeat them as many times as you like, for example applying a series of effects to some text to create your own style. This is like a customisable version of Recipes, and relieves boredom as well as saving time.

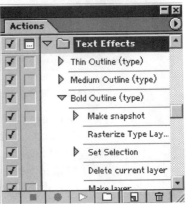

Paths Palette

Photoshop 6 includes significantly more advanced vector (line) graphic tools, allowing you to create your own shapes rather than simply using pre-defined ones. These can be very advantageous when creating web graphics.

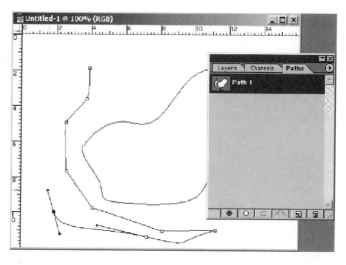

Other Features

As well as the alternate palettes, Photoshop 6 has a number of extended features accessed through fuller palettes and menu options.

Layer Styles

The Layer Styles dialog in Photoshop 6 is far more complex than the one on Elements, allowing the user to make a number of changes to each layer style applied. Not only that, but the changes can be made independently of each other, as each style has its own page in the dialog box.

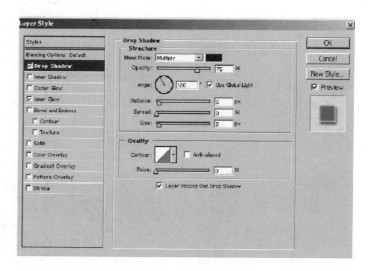

Masking

Photoshop 6 includes a number of different masking techniques to make it easier to work on a single area of an image, or to create effects. This includes a quick mask, accessible from the toolbar, and some more advanced options that work using the layers palette.

Comments

Photoshop 6 also includes some features designed to help more than one user complete a task, including the ability to save comments on areas of the picture much like using Post-It™ notes.

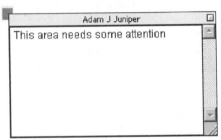

ImageReady

Photoshop 6 also includes a separate but integrated application for creating web-ready graphics. The slice tool in Photoshop allows you to cut an image up into sections that can become web pages, then you can swap over to ImageReady with one click. ImageReady works in a similar manner to Photoshop but with the tools and palettes laid out with the web in mind.

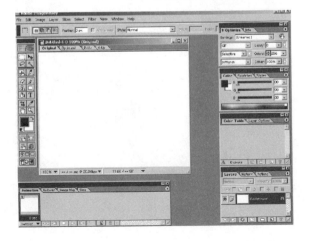

Why Photoshop 6?

In order to restore your home photos, paint pictures or prepare simple posters, there is really no need to change from Photoshop Elements. The bigger brother costs significantly more money and the extra features are, for the most part, complicated and unnecessary, especially if you only print to your home printer or maybe have Apple produce photo-albums for you.

Elements even includes some features that are not in Photoshop 6, like the File Browser, Red Eye Removal tool and Hints palette.

The main additional tools included in Photoshop 6 are for pre-press and internet work, so if you found yourself working in a professional context you would almost certainly need them. There are also more options and more controls in all the other tools, but these are luxuries. At the end of the day, you get a lot more for your $99 than you do for the extra $510.

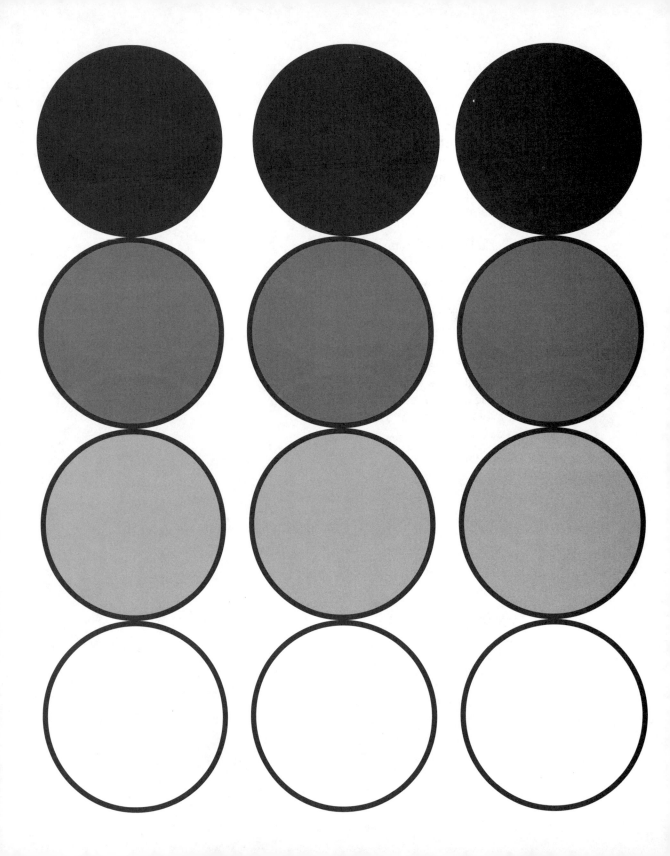

APPENDIX B KEYBOARD SHORTCUTS

Once you become familiar with a program, you start to want to speed up your work. In common with many other applications, Photoshop Elements has an array of keyboard shortcuts. Some of them are even easier to remember than in a word processor because you're not always typing text so there is less need for Ctrl/⌘ keys. In this appendix, we've summarised some of the most useful ones for you.

Mac Controls

In this section (for reasons of clarity on the diagrams) the PC shortcuts have been given. Mac users should strike the Command (⌘) key where PC users are told to use their Ctrl key. For example:

- Ctrl-S = ⌘-S

- Ctrl-Shift-S = ⌘-Shift-S

Main Controls

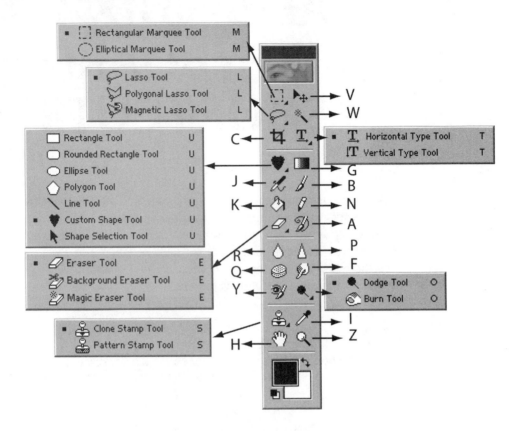

Pressing the Shift key as you press the letter (for those tools which hide behind each other) cycles through the 'hidden' tools. If you just press the letter key it will select the most recently used tool (which is visible in the Toolbox).

Shortcut Bar

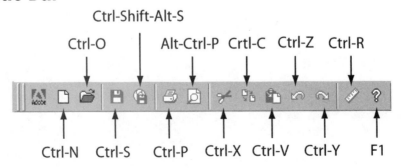

Document Navigation

To quickly use the Zoom or Hand tools without changing from the tool you're working with.

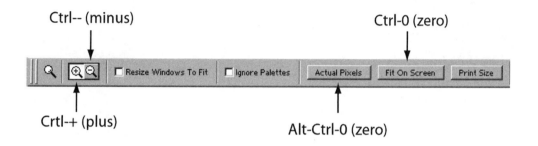

Ctrl-- (minus)

Crtl-+ (plus)

Ctrl-0 (zero)

Alt-Ctrl-0 (zero)

Hold the Space Bar

Hold Ctrl-Space

Hold Ctrl-Alt-Space

- Scroll up one window size – Page Up

- Scroll down one window size – Page Down

- Scroll left one window size – Ctrl-Page Up

- Scroll right one window size – Ctrl-Page Down

- Hide (and show again) selected pixels – Ctrl-H

- Go to upper left hand corner – Home

- Go to bottom right hand corner – End

Selection Controls

You can also:

Alt-[Any Selection Tool]

Shift-Alt-[Any Selection Tool]

Shift-[Any Selection Tool]

- Deselect – Ctrl-D

- Feather an Area – Ctrl-Alt-D

- Invert selected area – Ctrl-Shift-I

- Use the cursor (arrow) keys to move selection areas or shapes around, one pixel at a time.

- When using the Magnetic Lasso tool, pressing + increases the detection area.

Painting

Shift-[+ or -] to cycle through

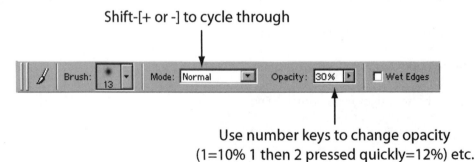

Use number keys to change opacity
(1=10% 1 then 2 pressed quickly=12%) etc.

- With any painting or shape tool selected, hold Alt for the Eyedropper () tool.

- Toggle lock transparent pixels – /

- Holding shift when painting and clicking draws a straight line between points.

Text

Ctrl-L Ctrl-R

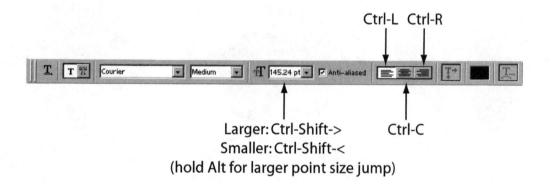

Larger: Ctrl-Shift->
Smaller: Ctrl-Shift-<
(hold Alt for larger point size jump)

Ctrl-C

- Underline – Ctrl-Shift-U

- Strikethrough – Ctrl-Shift-/

- Select one character at a time – Shift-[Arrow Key in direction you wish to select]

- New Test tool start point – Shift-Click

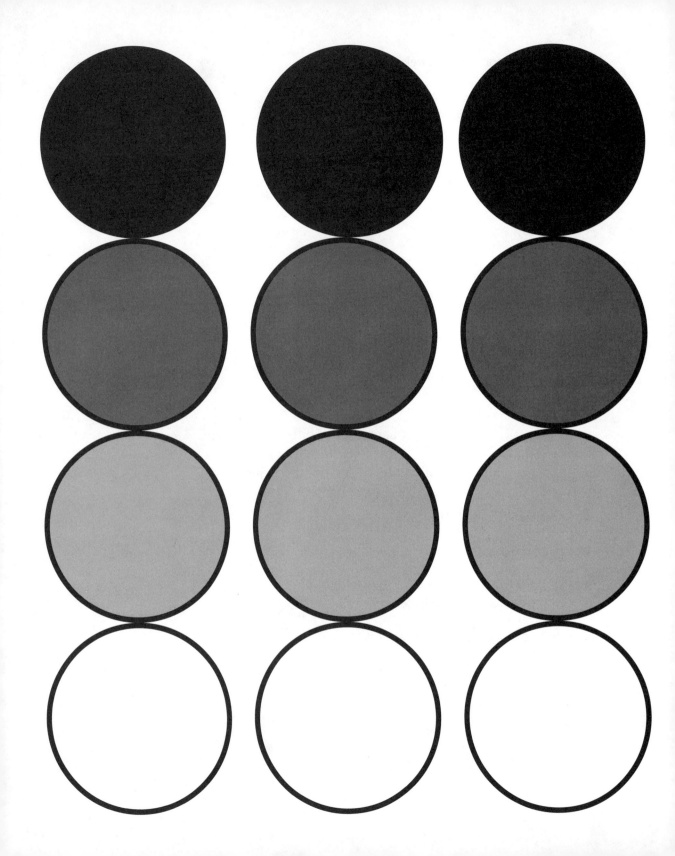

INDEX

The index is arranged hierarchically, in alphabetical order, with symbols preceding the letter A. Many second-level entries also occur as first-level entries. This is to ensure that users will find the information they require however they choose to search for it.

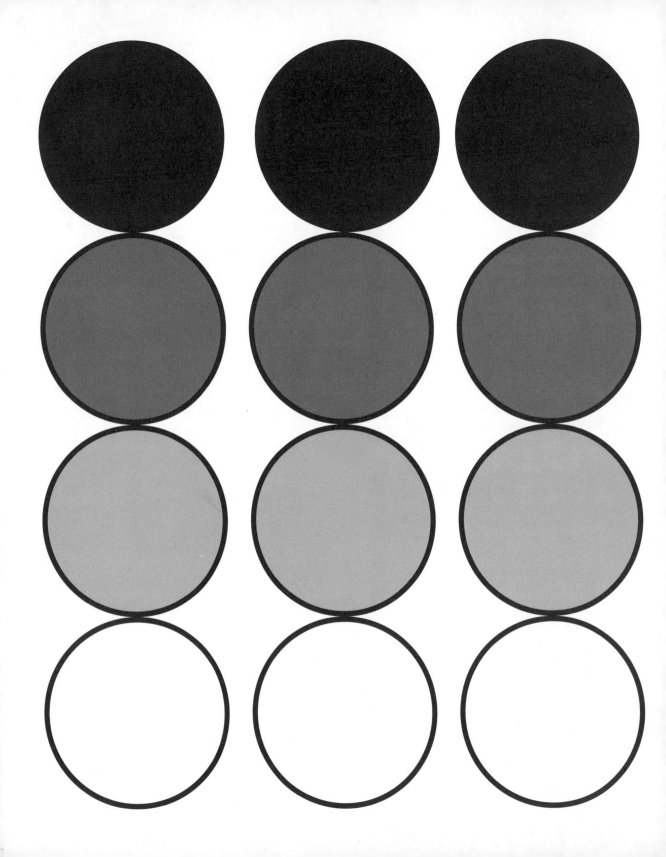

Notes

Notes